What Happened
When Show Business
Married the Mafia

Larry Spellman
& Sesh Heri

Jaguar Press

WHAT HAPPENED WHEN SHOW BUSINESS MARRIED THE MAFIA

Copyright 2013 By Larry Spellman & Sesh Heri

Inquiries should be addressed to:

Jaguar Press

Larryspellman9@gmail.com

Palm Springs, CA

FIRST PUBLICATION MARCH 2014

Cover Art: Walter Bosley & Robert Harkins

Published in the United States of America

Prologue

I was at the Mardi Gras Club in Baltimore on business for William Morris when the owner, Vince Bonalis, asked me to do him a favor. Since he was barred from ever entering Pimlico Racetrack, he gave me $2,000 to go to the track and just bet the #2 horse in the 5th race...obviously the fix was in!

Having time to kill until the race, I treated myself to a shave at the track's barbershop. The shop was filled with guys studying racing forms and shooting the breeze with horseflesh odds and statistics. My turn came and I got in the chair.

"Are you from around here?" my barber asked. "And how's the track? Been good to you so far?"

"I'm from New York," I said, "and I'm only here to bet just one horse in the fifth race."

You had to see how all the other guys got up from their chairs to turn and look at me—- a picture worth all the money Vince Bonalis was about to score!

That's a sample of the life I was living. But it wasn't even the least of it. What do I mean by that?

Well...let me explain....

CHAPTER ONE

Mailroom 1959

That Monday morning never felt so good. It was early November 1959...

I was riding the New York subway, the Independent Line that ran from my home in the Bronx down into midtown Manhattan. I knew this line well, had ridden it many times. I knew its smells on hot damp days and on days when it was pouring rain. In those days there was no air conditioning to moderate the temperature extremes of the New York seasons. The heat and the damp and the closeness of the other riders let you know who was next to you. To say we were packed in like sardines would be an understatement. We were the great American melting pot, now fused together into one compact mass. That's why the lyrics to the song Sinatra made famous are so true: If you can make it in New York, you can make it *anywhere*.

Those words in Sinatra's song were especially true for me this day in November, 1959. At that time, New York City was the geographic center of the world's media. Although the Golden Age of Hollywood had already faded into a Technicolor sunset, network television production had still not shifted its center of gravity to the West Coast. It was still here in New York where many television shows were created and broadcast. Supporting the television productions was the whole advertising industry, most of it ranged out along Madison Avenue. Then there were the great Broadway theatres, charged with the electric tension of mid-century literary genius. This was the era of Inge and Miller. It was a time when writers knew how to write and actors knew how to act. And it was the age of great entertainers who had earned their Ph.D.s in the school of hard knocks, performing upon the boards of countless vaudeville and nightclub stages.

It was into this incredible city of talent, ability, know-how, and opportunity that I now hurtled on the subway. I was going to my first day of a new job for me in Manhattan, and, despite the huddled masses hurtling along with me, my mind was racing so fast thinking about what lay ahead that I didn't even notice that there was anybody riding on that train with me. It was just me barreling into New York—- a town so exciting that, even if you're standing still, you're doing it at 22 miles an hour.

When the train stopped at the 57th Street station I pushed past all the people and stepped through the train's doors. It was like coming up inside a geyser under pressure. Everybody around me was pushing their way out too. We all streamed on to the platform and then rapidly overflowed the stairs to the street level above. Then we were on the street—- no longer subway passengers going to New York—- but now New Yorkers ourselves, rushing forth as the tide of a single river. I suddenly cut through this flow, making my own path. I knew where I was going.

I was headed for the Mutual of New York building on Broadway between 56th and 55th Streets. In this building on three of its floors were located the offices of the William Morris Agency—- the greatest theatrical agency in the world. It was here at William Morris where I had landed my job. Everything I had ever done in my life up to this moment had prepared me for this, my great opportunity.

My walk from the train station to the Mutual of New York building was the fastest I ever made. In a city where everyone walks fast, I cut past person after person. I strode on to Broadway, making sprinters look like turtles. The city opened before me, folding aside as I moved forward. Traffic sounds seemed a hailing signal. The buildings and the streets and the people seemed more alive to me than on any other day of my life. Suddenly the door of the Mutual building was before me, and I went through it in a flash.

In the lobby I slowed my pace, crossing the floor with assurance, and entered the open door of an elevator. I punched the button for the 32nd floor and started moving up into the building.

When the elevator doors opened on the 32nd floor, I moved toward a space in which floated the huge WMA logo. An instant later I realized that the logo was attached to the wall behind the reception desk. My glance moved over the logo and a tingle shot up my spine. This was what I had been dreaming about my entire four years at NYU.

"Yes?"

The voice was female, cool, and poised ready to drip with contempt. I looked over and saw that the voice belonged to the receptionist, a blonde with ice-blue eyes.

"I'm Larry Spellman," I said, smiling into all her ice, "here to start my first day on the job."

"What job?" she asked flatly.

"In the mailroom," I said.

"Oh," she said, still cool, as if my information barely qualified as information. "It's down the hall there. See Sherman Tankel."

"Tankel?" I asked.

She barely nodded once. I guessed that's how they did it in the northern climes.

"Thanks," I said.

All that ice didn't even blink.

Having made my Big Impression, I went down the hall, not waiting for any further expressions of admiration from the receptionist. I figured she was just a little slow from all those long days up there by the Arctic Circle.

I made my way down the hallway, which was laid out in a kind of horseshoe configuration. I was soon sure that I had the right place because of the clue on the wall by an entryway: a sign that read "Mailroom." I stepped through the entryway and looked about inside.

It was a not very big room containing tables stacked with boxes of mail, metal canisters of film, and a few city directories and telephone books. In the center of the room was a table with an upright box sitting on it. The box had a series of little slots in which to place mail. Next to the postal box was a Pitney-Bose postal meter machine. Off to one side, sitting on a table, was another machine, a mimeograph. Directly facing me was a glass caged office with a desk and telephone inside; this was a place where the head of the mailroom could talk on the phone in quiet, and talk to trainees a bit louder. Off to my left, as I came into the room, a guy sat at a semi-circular desk, talking on the telephone. I later learned that he was the dispatcher. Sitting at the tables were several guys dressed in suits just like I was. They were looking through pieces of mail and putting them into some kind of stacked order on the tables.

Nobody looked up from their work, so I just said, "I'm Larry Spellman here to see Sherman Tankel."

A heavy-set, jowly guy about 24 years old suddenly looked up at me. Below his chin were two more chins. This was the kind of guy who probably looked old when he was in kindergarten.

"Spellman?" the heavy-set guy asked.

"Been expecting you. I'm Sherman Tankel."

Sherman Tankel stood up and looked at his watch.

"You're on time," he said, "but around here we start as early as we can. You'll see. Come on in here."

Sherman Tankel led me in to the glass caged office and indicated a chair. I sat down in it, and he went and sat behind the desk.

"Spellman, Larry," he read from a sheet of paper on the desk. "I see you here. When did you interview?"

"Last Thursday, Mr. Tankel," I replied.

"Sherman," he said. "Call me Sherman. I'm not the head of the mailroom. I'm just a trainee like you, filling in until they get someone permanent. So here it is. The job is from nine to five some days and other days eleven to seven and Saturday mornings once a month. I'll give you the schedule later today. The salary is fifty a week. I guess they already told you that."

"Oh, yes," I said.

"I know," Sherman said. "That salary level is a little hard to swallow. Lucky if you can swallow anything on fifty a week. Everybody here has outside income: weekend jobs or they live at home with their parents or—- the lucky ones—- the trust babies. How about you?"

"Weekend job," I said.

"Figured you for a weekend job," Sherman said. "Doing what?"

"I'm a musician," I said.

"Really," Sherman said. "What's your instrument?"

"Saxophone," I said.

"And they pay you to play?" Sherman asked.

"Dances, weddings, bar mitzvahs," I said, nodding. "I can clear a hundred a week."

"Dollars?" Sherman asked.

"And then I book a few bands," I said.

"And on this you make money too?" Sherman asked.

"I take my ten percent," I said. "I do all

13

right."

"You think you can do all that and work here full time?" Sherman asked.

"Sure," I said. "Why not?"

"Most of us here are not so...uh...preoccupied," Sherman said. "But—-okay, so you've got your outside job. Now I'll show you your job *here*."

Sherman stood up and so did I.

"Sorting mail," I said.

"Uh—- not just yet," Sherman said. "You're the new man, so right now you're low man on the totem pole. That means you have a very...uh...*special*...job."

"I'm ready for anything," I said. "Tell me all about it."

"Oh," Sherman said, "I'm going to *show* it to you. Come on."

Sherman led me out of the glass caged office and through the door of the mailroom. He took me down the hall, talking all the while to me in a low, even, carefully modulated voice. Every time someone approached in the hall, Sherman would stop speaking until they passed. He began:

"Every second you're in these halls you have to be on your best behavior. I saw on the paper that you've been in the army, so you know what I'm talking about. This is like the army, only more. You have to look your best at all times, hair combed, tie straight, pants pressed. See how straight the part is in my hair? One of the top agents combs his hair like this. Found out the name of his barber and now I go to the same place. It's expensive, but worth it. See how things go and maybe I'll tell you the barber's name. Now keep your eyes about you at all times. Speak only if spoken to and then it's, 'Yes, Mr. So-and-so. Right away, Mr. So-and-so.' Sh!"

A very nicely dressed older man approached us in the hall, looking down at some papers in his hand. In a moment he passed us and was out of sight.

"Who was that?" I asked.

"Who was that?" Sherman repeated. "You

don't know?"

"No," I said.

"That was Nat Kalcheim," Sherman said.

I stopped and looked back up the hall where the man had disappeared around a corner.

"That was *him*?" I asked.

"That was *him*," Sherman said solemnly. "One of the founding fathers of the William Morris Agency.   Sort of like walking past George Washington, huh?"

"Yeah," I said, "only better."

"You see what I mean about how it is in these halls?" Sherman asked.

"I see what you mean," I said.

We started along the hall again.   Sherman resumed his orientation lecture:

"So don't chat with anybody.   Don't loaf around the water cooler.   Don't try to make time with the receptionists.   Don't put your hands in your pockets."

I took my hands out of my pockets. Sherman stopped in the hall and looked at me.

"You're ready for anything," Sherman said. "Welcome to anything."

Sherman pushed a door open and we went through it and stepped into the men's room.

"Oh," I said, "I'm sorry. I didn't realize. I'll just wait for you outside."

"Come back here," Sherman said. "I didn't come in here to pee. This is where you'll be working from now on."

I stopped on the threshold, holding the door open.

"What?" I asked.

I hadn't understood what Sherman had just said. It wouldn't fit into my brain.

"The men's room," Sherman said. "This is your new job."

I slowly stepped into the men's room, closing the door behind me.

"You're kidding," I said. "You've got to be kidding."

"And where on my face are you seeing the smile?" Sherman asked. "Everybody starts out right here—- in Flushing, New York. Everybody."

"Sherman," I said, "I have a Bachelor of Science degree from NYU."

"Yes, I know," Sherman said. "Very impressive. Saw that on your application. But let me inform you: everybody here has a university degree. And we all started out right here in the men's room—- doing paperwork."

"Paperwork?" I asked.

Sherman went to a cabinet and opened its door. Inside were stacks of toilet paper rolls. He removed one of the rolls and carried it to a toilet stall.

"Paperwork," Sherman said. "No job is finished until the paperwork is done. And I see here that the last guy didn't finish his paperwork. We'll do it for him and keep his name out of it. He's lucky we found it and not someone else."

I looked into where Sherman stood in the stall. He was removing an empty cardboard tube from the spring-loaded toilet paper bar and replacing it with the new roll of toilet paper. He got the new roll on the bar and snapped it back into place.

"The tissue rolls from the top down, not the bottom under," Sherman observed. "Remember that. This is your new job from now on."

"You're serious," I said.

"Top down, Larry," Sherman said. "That's the way everything is done around here—- from the top down. Got it?"

"Got it," I said.

"Toilet paper is very important around here," Sherman said.

"Around anywhere," I said, shrugging.

Sherman grimaced at me.

"An agent came in here one time," Sherman said, "and there was no toilet paper in the stall. Guess what happened to the trainee who was assigned to the men's room?"

"He got fired?" I guessed.

"Fired?" Sherman repeated. "He was never seen or heard from again."

"From anybody?" I asked.

19

"Not in show business," Sherman said. "Maybe his mother heard something."

Sherman flushed the toilet.

"You can go down quick around here, Larry, if you don't do your paperwork," Sherman said. "Understand?"

"I understand," I said.

"Now this assignment is not just the toilet paper," Sherman said.

"I didn't think it would be," I said.

"It's the paper towels and the soap dispenser as well," Sherman said. "You've got to keep us in soap. Soap...soap gives hope. That is, it gives *you* hope that you'll keep your job."

"What about the floors?" I asked. "Am I going to have to make a consultation with Mr. Clean?"

"Cute," Sherman said. "The janitors do the floors. You're not the janitor."

"Oh, no," I said. "I'm the men's room attendant—- college entry level."

"Say that with pride, Lare," Sherman said.

"But if somebody makes a mess and you can't locate the janitor right away, guess who gets an opportunity to prove his executive potential?"

"Little ol' me," I said.

"Bingo," Sherman said.

"And all I have to do is this and I pile up fifty smackers a week?" I asked.

"Oh," Sherman said, "this just starts your day off with a sparkle. You take care of this first fast as you can and then beat it back to the mailroom. Come on. I have a job for you right now."

"Oh, boy!" I exclaimed. "Paperwork!"

"Not paperwork," Sherman said. "Come on."

Sherman took me back to the mailroom. When we got there, he stopped in front of the table with the stacks of film canisters.

"These are kinescopes," Sherman said, "motion picture footage made with a camera set up in front of a television screen. These are all films of shows made by our clients. I want you to shlep these two cans over to this advertising agency on Madison Avenue."

Sherman handed me the agency's business card.

"Here's two dollars for cab fare," Sherman said. "Sign for the money."

I signed a receipt, and then took the two bills that Sherman held out in his hand.

"We usually walk and pocket the two dollars," Sherman said.

"At fifty a week, I'll walk," I said.

"I should tell you, though," Sherman said, "these cans can get heavy."

I picked up the two cans of film by their handles, one in each of my hands.

"These things?" I asked. "They're light as a feather."

"Well, then," Sherman said, "you ought to be able to fly over there."

"Cute," I said. I went to the door, carrying the cans in each of my hands.

"Look fellas," Sherman said, "he just floated

across the room!   You're going to need some ballast, Larry!"

"Yeah," I said, "but from the looks of your belt size, I can see you won't."

The other trainees burst out laughing.

"See ya, Lare," Sherman said.

"See ya, Sherman," I said.

Then Sherman grinned. He could dish it out and take it, too. And he could see that I could do the same.

I started out the door of the mailroom carrying the film cans by their handles. When I got to the elevators, I stopped and looked over to the receptionist who I had spoken to earlier, the one with the ice-blue eyes. I smiled and held up the film canisters. Still, she didn't even blink. The elevator doors opened and I went through them, hoping for some warmer air.

Down below on the sidewalks of Broadway I looked up at the sky. I hadn't noticed it before on my way to the WMA offices. The sky was gray and darker than when I had first arrived in Manhattan that morning. I started down Broadway on foot, carrying a film canister in each hand, grasping them by their handles. I was only wearing my suit without a top coat. As I walked, I noticed a sprinkling of rain on the sidewalk.

By the time I made it to Fifth Avenue the sprinkles had turned to a downpour and my suit and hair were beginning to get soaked. I looked for a cab, but saw not a one in all the snarl of traffic before me. The way the cars were creeping along right then I wondered if two dollars would even cover the fare to Madison Avenue anyway. I kept to my course on foot. The film cans were now getting heavy. If they were feathers, they were feathers made of lead. By the time I got to Madison Avenue I thought my arms would fall off. I kept walking. I was getting drenched, and the wind had raked my hair askew. I no longer looked my best.

What am I doing here, I wondered? I thought about that trainee Sherman had mentioned who had botched his men's room assignment and was never heard from again. What if I made a slight mistake and got fired and was never heard from again either? Then all of this menial drudgery would have amounted to nothing—- a total loss.

My feet kept walking in a straight line, but my mind kept going back over the same ground: What am I doing here? How did I ever get into this? How did it all start? I kept coming up with the same answer. It all started when *I* started. It all started with...*my very first memory.*

CHAPTER TWO

The Law Is Formed

It was a BRIGHT RED RING.

That was my very *first* memory. Let me explain.

When I was three years old, my mother would go over to Eighth and Bathgate Avenues in the Bronx and shop in the outdoor stalls. Mr. Moscowitz sold pants and knickers there. I remember that he used to measure things not with a yardstick or ruler, but with a rope knotted at intervals along its length. In another stall, Molly "the Chicken Lady" sold chickens with their legs always bound together by a ring, and not just any old ordinary ring, either. The rings were always a bright color: red, yellow, blue, green. We kids loved them. We would take the rings and put them on our fingers, real treasure. And that was my very first memory: one of the Chicken Lady's rings on my finger, a bright red one.

I had my hand held up in the air, the fingers of my hand spread out, with that red ring on my third finger. Over the top of the red ring I could see my mother's head, sticking out of a window on the fourth floor of our building. Her mouth was open and she was yelling down to me while I was yelling up to her.

I had-- and have-- no idea as to the specifics of what she was saying. I wasn't really listening to her. But I know it was some emphatic form of, "No, I won't!" or, "No, you can't!" I was yelling back to her, "Gimme it! Gimme it!"

"It" was a nickel. This was 1939 when a nickel bought a pound of potatoes and ten cents a quart of milk. I remember somehow that at this point my mother had already just given me *two* nickels, so a third nickel was out of the question. But I kept insisting.

You see, every so often, the pony ride man

would come around to our neighborhood. He charged a nickel a ride. So every time he would come while I was playing out on our street, I would yell from the sidewalk up to the fourth floor window of the building where we lived for my mother to throw me down a nickel. She would stick her head out and throw down a nickel wrapped in a napkin. Then I would yell again for her to throw me down another nickel for a second ride, which she would do reluctantly. When the time came for me to get my *third* ride, my mother was more than reluctant to part with that third nickel. She was the Rock of Gibraltar. No third nickel. Too much money.

This was what was happening now. She was doing her Rock of Gibraltar impression, and doing it very well, if the Rock of Gibraltar had an open mouth repeating, "No, no, no!"

You know what I did to be spiteful? I lay down in the middle of the gutter, not letting any cars go by, and cursed with every four letter word I knew at the top of my lungs. I lay there and cursed, and had no intention of letting up until I got my nickel. I think this time I got the nickel. But this happened several times, and sometimes I'd get the nickel, but sometimes I'd get the strap, especially if my father was around.

My father was very strict and didn't hesitate to use the strap when I got out of line. But even then I did things my own way. Sometimes if somebody I didn't like walked down the sidewalk in front of our building, I would stand at our fourth floor window, take aim, and pee on them. If my father found out, it was the strap. But that didn't stop me from keeping look-out at the window, and being quick on the draw. My father was very strict about enforcing rules at meal time, too. If we broke those rules, it was the strap. But still, I would go right ahead and eat dinner my own way.

For instance, we were supposed to wash our hands before dinner. Once I didn't want to. My father grabbed me, pushed me into the bathroom, and forcefully washed my hands. You know what I did, even though I knew the strap was coming? I lay down, and ran my hands all over the floor to dirty them again.

Yet, I loved my parents, regardless of the punishments they dished out because I knew that I deserved those punishments. And, strange to say, I felt their love in the punishments, because it was clear to me that they cared about what I did and what I was. I was important enough to them for them to take up their time and effort in punishing me. And I took up a lot of their time and effort. Like the time and effort they expended upon me the day I got my friends together and said, "Let's go to the Bronx Zoo."

Keep in mind that on the day this happened I was still only three years old. This was a time in our country's history when three year old kids could play in the streets outside their houses and apartments without any reason for their parents to be concerned for their safety. It was a different time then, a different world.

Neighborhoods were safe then. If somebody got mugged, all the newspapers would carry the story as if it was a major event. The only serious crimes that existed were gangland murders committed amongst members of the gangs themselves. In fact, the crime families that lived in the respective boroughs protected their neighborhoods. These were families like the East Harlem mob headed by Lucky Luciano, the Gambino and the Columbo mobs in Brooklyn, and the Dutch Schultz mob in my neighborhood in the east Bronx where I lived until I was five years old. A woman could walk down the street late at night and not worry about it. The cop on the beat was no small factor contributing to that safety. He had that club always swaying in one hand and that gun always noticeable on his belt. These were the days before civilian review boards existed, so when you saw that cop coming around the corner, you practically stood at attention.

Now the day I said, "Let's go to the Bronx Zoo," is a day I'll never forget. Looking back now seventy-one years later, I can't believe what I did on that day! I was only three years old! When I see a three-year old now, I see a little, helpless child. On that day when I was a three year old, I was hell-bent for adventure. And talk about adventure, this was it! I cooked up the whole thing in my own head early that day as I stood outside my apartment with the members of my gang. Yes, three year-olds had gangs in those days. The girls had their own groups, I suppose, but they played among themselves. Girls were allowed to come out and play at a young age also, but they had to stay right in front of their building, or the building next door. The boys could wander up and down our block, Fulton Avenue. We could also play in the big city park across the street, Crotona Park, as long as we were still in view of our buildings. Of course, all the houses on our block being tenements, you would, from time to time, see mothers sticking their heads out the windows, double-checking on us. Every mother looked out for every other mother's kids...neighbors were truly neighborly!

On this day the mothers were not as attentive as usual. Maybe they were busy with some big event, I can't remember. But I remember looking up and noticing that nobody was looking down.

"Hey," I said.

My gang stood before me. There were several boys, none more than four years of age. We could all walk, talk, fight, and cuss. The boys all looked at me, and seemed to have some expectation that I had something to say that was worth the listening. There was Julius and Sam who lived in my building. And there was a black kid called "Peachy" who was the son of the superintendent of the building next to ours. There were several other boys: a kid with a cap whose name I no longer remember, a round-faced kid, a very little kid whose pants were always about to fall down (since he wore his older brother's clothes), and several more boys whose faces and names have faded from my memory. But as a group, I remember them well, and remember them standing there, legs spread

33

apart like soldiers or cowboys or pirates about to go out on a raid.

"Let's go to the Bronx Zoo," I said. The idea had been simmering in my mind for several minutes. The ingredients were those empty windows over our heads, the empty park across the street where we had already explored so many times before and vague memories of a trip to the Bronx Zoo with my father where he had rushed us through before we could get a satisfactory eyeful of all the sights.

I could see in my mind's eye the direction in which the Bronx Zoo lay. I could see the many intervening city blocks that lay between me and it. But spanning that space was the Third Avenue elevator train. The train would take us there. Money? Who needed money when all you had to do was sneak on! Just get on the train, and, at the end of the line, we'd only be about ten blocks from the entrance of the zoo! We could walk that far! The magic of seeing and then doing.

"The Bronx Zoo!" Julius exclaimed.

34

"That's far."

"That's a hundred miles," Sam said.

"It's way up in Alaska," Julius said.

"It's that way," I said, pointing north-east. "Let's go."

I turned and started walking. The rest of my gang followed me without further comment. We were going to the zoo and that was that. The boys had complete faith in my judgment and knowledge. They were sure that if I said we'd get there, we would. And because I was sure, they didn't have to be bothered with any doubts of their own.

We got to the Third Avenue station, and sneaked through the turnstiles and on to the train. Its doors closed, we sat down, and watched the Bronx tenements move past us. Some of the boys had never seen this part of the neighborhood before, and they kept their heads turned to the windows. Some of them had their noses actually *stuck* to the windows.

Julius kept watching the city go by. In a while he said, "This train's going a *lot* further than

35

Alaska. We're going to the North Pole!"

"No we ain't," Sam said. "The North Pole's the other way-- way over in Brooklyn."

"When I get to the zoo," Julius said, "I'm going to shoot a bear."

"No you ain't," Sam said. "They don't put bears in zoos. They're too mean. They just got wild animals there."

"How you know?" Julius asked.

"I got a big zoo book with pictures," Sam said, "and there ain't no bears in it. But it's got pictures of elephants in it. They're big as a truck!"

We got to the end of the last stop on the line, Fordham Road, the premiere shopping street in the Bronx. If you had a very special occasion and really wanted to dress up, you went to Fordham Road, perhaps spending as much as $29 for a pair of fancy shoes. We got off the train there and strolled by all the store windows, sometimes stopping and peering in at the beautiful dresses, gowns and tuxedos. We then kept walking onward, about ten blocks east to the entrance of the zoo, and sneaked inside.

Once inside, we made our way slowly along the walkways. We got to the elephants and I pointed them out to the other boys.

"That's an elephant," I said.

"It's bigger than a truck," Sam said.

"It's bigger than a house," Julius said.

"It's big as a mountain this high," Sam said raising his arm and going up on tiptoes.

Suddenly the elephant gushed out a fire-hose volume of urine.

"I wouldn't want to get under that!" Sam said. "These animals are all wild."

We laughed and held our noses, and then ran off, all wild ourselves.

We went through the whole zoo, and the whole zoo seemed to go through all of us. We felt the place and took in the place as only three-year olds could do. We jumped and ran and climbed up on fences and railings and yelled. We got our money's worth without paying any money. We stayed quite a while. And when we left, we weren't thrown out. We walked out, just like all the paying customers.

Outside the gate of the zoo, Sam asked, "What time is it?"

"It's about a billion o'clock," Julius said.

The sun was on the tree-tops.

"I want to go home!" Sam said.

"Me too," Julius said. "I'm hungry."

"I'm tired," Sam said.

"Come on," I said.

Once again, the boys fell in line. They were laying their cares all on me. Well, I did know how to get home. I had thought it all out before I left. In those days, on strategic corners of different streets there were small, pyramid-like structures that housed transfers that bus drivers gave to riders who had to transfer to another bus to complete their journey. Those days, for a 5 cent fare you got those free transfers.

I had a good idea where one of those pyramid-like structures was located, and I led the other boys to it. When we got to it, we all stopped and looked up at it.

"Up there," I said. "If we get up there and break that lock, we can get bus tickets!"

One of us climbed up on another's shoulders, broke the lock, and took the transfers we needed. That got us on the bus heading south to Crotona Parkway. If you used a transfer to get on the bus, you could not get another transfer, which meant that when we got off the bus we had to walk west through the park at night and in the rain to get back to Fulton Avenue.

Just before we got to the avenue, I suddenly saw my oldest brother approaching. He came up to me and kicked me in my butt. Then I saw my mother and father—- and the mothers and fathers of all the boys in our gang! They were out in force looking for us. I later learned that they also had the police out looking for us. Don't forget that the gang of which I was the ringleader was only 3 to 4 years old!

Do I have to tell you how hard my father's strap was when we got upstairs into the apartment?

But instead of this putting an end to my adventures, it only whetted my appetite for more. I wanted to see more, do more, and all in my own way, on my own terms. It took my father a while to figure out that I had my own way of doing things, a way that wasn't necessarily bad, just different from what he knew.

My father, Morris Spellman, started it all (me) when, in 1912, he came to America from Bessarabia, an eastern European country that was annexed after World War I by either Romania or Russia (nobody remembers today). He came here to America by way of England where he had relatives and with whom he lived for three years. My father's real family name was Catrosa, but he adopted his relatives' name, which was Spillman. That was our name until I was four years old. Then my father changed our name to Spellman. At that time, one of the most powerful clerics in the United States was Cardinal Spellman, head of the archdiocese of New York; he could get President

Franklin Delano Roosevelt on the phone if he wanted to. Everybody confused our last name with his and used to call us Spellman instead of Spillman, so my father changed it officially.

Annie Brookmeyer (later cut to Brooks) was my mother. She and her sister Esther came over here to America from Austria in 1913 at their brother, Harry's insistence, who came here first. Growing up, we all called Esther by her inherited nickname, Dunya.

My mother, Dunya, and their brother Harry grew up on a big farm in Austria. Compulsory education existed in Austria and they were well educated. Eastern European countries' educational systems were usually reserved for those who could afford it. Otherwise, one's learning came from the local rabbi, if you were Jewish. The rest of the boys coming out of elementary school went to work doing whatever their father did. My mother was always so proud of becoming an American. She always said, "In Europe, if your father was a shoemaker, then you would become a shoemaker.

In America, a man might be a shoemaker, grocery clerk or farmer, but his sons will go on to become doctors, lawyers, engineers."

My mother and Dunya landed in America at Boston Harbor. From there they went up to Fall River, Massachusetts. It was my Uncle Harry who introduced my mother to my father and Nathan Abramowitz to Dunya. They all married almost on the same day.

Fall River attracted a lot of European immigrants because the mills that made fabric were centralized there and work was plentiful. This was before the ascendancy of the unions, which caused the mills to close down and move to the South. The town dried up when that happened.

My father, being a tailor, moved with my mother and by then my sister Essie (their first born) and my brother Herbert to New York where he knew that his skills would lend themselves to him getting a job in the garment center. My parents first moved to Brooklyn for a short while, and it was there that my brother Jerry was born. Things were so rough financially that Jerry's crib was one of the draws of a clothing chest. The Bronx came next where my brother Robby was born. Then seven years later (in other words I was an accident) my journey began. So there we were, a big American family, my mother, father, a sister, three brothers––and finally me, the baby of the family, who, true to my character, sneaked in while no one was looking.

Things were different in 1936 when I was born at Morrisania Hospital. You never heard of health insurance. Each borough had a city hospital. You paid what you could afford, and if you were broke, they still took you in. The quality of doctors was superb even in city hospitals. When my older brother Jerry and I were born we were "feet first." In those days it was almost a given that during this type of birth either the mother or the baby died. The hospital at no cost to my father brought in a top-notch doctor who saved both my mother and her babies.

Not only were our hospitals great, but also our public educational system was outstanding.

Other than Catholic schools or Yeshiva for Jewish kids, you never heard of kids going to private schools.

I was in 3rd grade at PS 70 in the west Bronx when my life's direction began. The school's music teacher, Mr. Tuttleman, wanted to encourage kids to think about learning a musical instrument. The city school system actually owned instruments that they loaned to students interested in taking music lessons. Mr. Tuttleman held a special music appreciation class showing us different instruments to see if a student would be attracted to one. The idea being if you started taking lessons from the recommended private teachers in the 3rd grade, by the time you were in the 5th grade you would be ready to join the school's orchestra.

I immediately gravitated to the clarinet, which the school loaned me. Saturday mornings my mother took me to Mr. Kreisberg, the private teacher for my lessons, which cost all of $2. My big treat was after the lesson my mother took me to the corner candy store where I got a huge chocolate malted and a salted pretzel. I really took to the clarinet, practiced every day after school and made good progress.

Both of my parents worked very hard. Like the other women in the East Bronx, my mother had one of those washboards that she would use to scrub the clothes soaking in the bathtub. She always wanted to make sure that we went to school nicely dressed. She used to do all the washing and ironing.

On Sundays, my father was so exhausted that he would just catch up on his sleep while my mother would take a couple of my brothers and me to Orchard Beach, near City Island. My brothers and I were all big swimmers. Even though I was young, I would go way out in the water. My mother would stand on the shore, waving and pointing a finger, yelling: "If you drown, Papa will kill you!"

My father kept working at his job in the garment district until I was nine and a half years old. Then he died, at the young age of 59. We were all shocked, but we all kept going, all of us pursuing our dreams, just as my father would have wanted us to do.

By the time I got to the 6th grade, I was in the school orchestra, playing in a concert of Victor Herbert's *Chocolate Soldier*. My mother was in the audience and Mr. Tuttleman asked me to stand up and play a solo. He said, "He looks like Benny Goodman and plays like Benny Goodman." Do I have to tell you how proud my mother was?

Jerry Weintraub, now the famous movie producer, played clarinet in the same orchestra. We also attended Jr. High School together. It was there where I got into a fist fight with him on the stairwell between classes. I was appointed as a monitor and stationed on a certain stairwell to make sure that students didn't linger. Jerry wouldn't stop talking at the top of his lungs, which was also prohibited. When he wouldn't stop—that's when the rumble happened. In later years we laughed about it when we renewed acquaintances during a time when I was an agent at William Morris and he was a personal manager representing such artists as Frankie Valli, Shelly Berman and Jane Morgan whom he eventually married.

It was while attending Bronx Jr. High 117 in ninth grade that my teacher, Miss Engle, stopped in front of me while I was standing in the doorway of a classroom. Maybe it was my way of blurting things out, or something about my sense of humor that made Miss Engle stop, look me up and down, look me in the eye, and then adjust my tie, while she said, with a faint smile, "Larry, you're a law unto yourself."

And then she walked away, leaving me standing there, thinking. It was the first time I could recall of anyone saying that about me, and it made me pause. You see, I always understood what she had said about me and I accepted myself as I was. I didn't think I was really a bad kid, just my own kid, that's all. But here was someone telling me that they understood this about me, and that it was all right. Miss Engle didn't say this about me in a way to imply that I should reform. She just said it as a simple observation of a fact that could not be changed. A law unto myself? Well, yes, but what did that *really* mean? To figure that out completely would take me a lifetime. It would involve understanding what laws were, how they were made, how they were kept, and how, sometimes, despite our best efforts, they're broken. But I knew there was something in me, something I called "the Law" that I could never break. It was some kind of code that I couldn't describe in words but knew perfectly well as a feeling that almost wasn't *in* me but *was* me. I would learn a lot along my life's pathway, and most of all I would learn that my way was not the *easy* way of going along to get along. I would learn that going my own way sometimes meant laying everything I had on the line, and then waiting for the roll of a pair of dice that weren't weighted in my favor.

What I'm describing is the path that any creative individual takes. Creative people—-artists, scientists, politicians, and yes, even businessmen of the entrepreneurial type-- never look for the kind of guarantees that most people do who punch a time-clock. The higher the level of creativity one achieves the higher one's level of risk. This was my path, for initially I defined myself as a musician. I loved music with a passion. But I also understood that the truly creative person knows how to take *calculated* risks. There is nothing creative about painting yourself into a corner. So it was in this frame of mind that I entered high school. And no ordinary high school for me, either. No, I went to the High School of Performing Arts, the school that they made the hit movie about, *FAME*.

The High School of Performing Arts was a relatively new school experiment run by the city, but ran like a professional high school. It was free to those dancers, actors and musicians who were able to pass a rigorous audition. It was located on 46th St. between Sixth and Seventh Avenues in Manhattan. There were only 600 students in the whole school. The building was actually an old warehouse that had been converted into classrooms, dance studios and rehearsal halls. Half a day was devoted to academics in case you were going on to college, and half a day you worked at your craft in order to further your skills. Besides an audition to get in, you had to reach a certain level of achievement every six months in order not to be dropped. To graduate you gave a recital.

By the time we did graduate, half the kids were already working professionals, particularly the musicians. I was accepted into the Musicians Union when I was just 15 years old. The   school was a real learning experience for me as to how crazy and different the world of show business is. I first began to see how "special" performers are. They're emotional, egotistical, self-centered and ambitious! This was good exposure for me as it prepared me for what was to come later on when I became an agent and had to handle performers with all their idiosyncrasies and child-like temperaments.

My very first experience of this was when on one of my first days at the school I was changing classes going down the stairwell. I saw a girl facing the wall, crying. I ran down to her as fast as I could and asked if there was something wrong. What a shock I got when she screamed at me, "Get away from me! You're ruining my scene!"

And I had thought musicians were nuts.

In this same atmosphere I completed my first booking. I was working in the orchestra pit of an off-Broadway musical when the conductor was unable to show up one night. I volunteered the services of one of my teachers and sold the producer on why Mr. Lash would be an excellent substitute conductor. What a thrill it was for me to be the middle man between the producer and the talent, which had never crossed my mind until then. The exhilaration stayed with me.

Not long after that I started booking bands for local special events. When a writer for the *Saturday Evening Post* was researching an article about high school kids working in show business, he found me and I became the focus of his story. What got him was when he asked me how I found talent and how I was able to book them. He quoted my answer in the article, "You gotta hustle, man, you gotta hustle." How true it was!

51

In preparation for our summer vacations while at Performing Arts I would put a band together, audition for agents, and get booked at one of the hundreds of hotels that flourished in the Catskill Mountains, just a two hour car ride north of New York City.

The Catskills started out as a number of not very successful farms around the turn of the twentieth century. The farmers started taking in relatives and friends from New York when they would come up to visit on their summer vacations. In a few years the farms had turned into rustic vacation resorts, and farming went by the wayside. The Catskills really started blossoming with hotel growth around the late 1920s as a place for Jewish garment center workers to go with their families and get out of the heat for a week or two during the summers. As more and more hotels were built catering to more and more people looking for a vacation that was close to New York, competition between hotel owners became fierce; they all wanted to outdo one another. What did they do?

They built little social halls that they called casinos (there wasn't any gambling, so I don't know how they came up with that), hired a band for the summer that played for dancing and showed movies on the band's night off. When that wasn't enough, they started to bring in shows, first on a Saturday night and then on multiple nights if the hotel got big enough. Usually a dance team, a comedian and a singer combined would make up the evening's entertainment. Some of the most famous stars from the late 1930s until the early '70s got their start this way. As time went on, some of the hotels evolved into major hotel complexes accommodating 1,000 to 3,000 guests. Indoor and outdoor swimming pools, riding stables and golf courses were all part of their offering. More important for me was that they started building actual showrooms. The Concord and Grossinger's were prime examples of the most prominent of these hotels.

After just two summers playing with my own band in smaller hotels, I was lucky enough to be hired by some of these big bands at these big hotels, including the Concord and Grossinger's.

Playing the musical accompaniment for these stars gave me an invaluable education to see what went over with different audiences and what didn't; why some performers did well and some didn't. The absorption of these common denominators no doubt added to my later ascendancy in the ranks of William Morris agents. The Musicians Union was very strong, so we slept in nice quarters, just two to a room, and ate in the same dining room as the guests. Most of the waiters and busboys were guys working their way through college. When I saw how hard they worked, and the conditions under which they lived, I used to thank my lucky stars that I practiced as hard as I did when I was a kid musician.

Besides making good money, most of which you sent home to your mother to save for you, fun and laughs permeated all summer long. Even though there were hundreds of bands working in the Catskills, the towns were so close together that most of us got to know each other. We would organize jam sessions after hours, and fix each other up with the single girls who came to the Catskills to meet "Mr. Right," and yes, party with some of the married women who were loose and fanciful during the middle of the week whose husbands only came up on weekends. The history of that era when the Catskills was at its height could fill volumes!

By the time I graduated from PA in June '54, Latin music was at its peak in New York. Tito Puente, Tito Rodriguez, La Playa Sextet, Machito were some of the more famous of these bands. If you went to the Palladium Ballroom on 53rd Street and Broadway on any given night you could see major Hollywood stars and celebrities dancing the Mambo and the Cha-cha-cha. If you didn't have a date on Saturday night, you and your friends would look at the newspaper ads on Friday to see where some of these hot Latin bands were playing at ballrooms around the city. For a $2 admission you would go and meet single girls and hopefully get their telephone numbers to make future dates.

So I was about 18 when I and two other

musicians decided to form a partnership and promote our own Latin dances. We did so well that on some Saturday nights we were promoting five dances simultaneously at different ballrooms. The thrill of negotiating with the agents of these Latin bands when hiring them, renting the ballrooms that were usually at hotels, getting city permits, working the advertising agencies to make sure your ads stood out in the newspapers—- and *especially* counting the ticket sales as the doors opened—- was absolutely *intoxicating*!

At the end of the summer after graduating from the High School of Performing Arts, I began attending the Manhattan School of Music on a flute scholarship. I could now play three different instruments and was concentrating on the tenor saxophone. Yet despite this, three months into my scholarship I realized that I was getting a greater thrill out of doing the business end of showbiz than I ever got out of playing music—- and don't forget that I had been playing since I was eight years old. I knew then and there that I wanted to be an agent!

I knew that if I was to have a shot at getting into the training program at one of the big agencies that dominated the field of entertainment, a music degree was not the right ticket. I needed a business degree. But how? I didn't have the money for another college. Welcome Uncle Sam. Late October 1954 I gave up my scholarship at the conservatory and joined the army. I could get the GI Bill to pay for my college education. A lot of guys made it through college this way. And believe me, we were all doing it the *hard* way.

Army.

Boot Camp.

BOOT CAMP.

Next to hell, one of the worst things that anybody could experience is ten weeks of basic training in the army. What kept me going was the knowledge that as bad as I had it, some Marine in his basic training was having it worse. Being someone like I am who is willing to assert himself when he thinks he's right just doesn't work well in army life.

Maneuvers.

MANEUVERS.

I don't even like the way that word looks, even in small case. It happened when we were on *maneuvers*. (Italics don't help either.)

It was January '55, the depth of winter in Fort Dix, New Jersey. We were sleeping on the ground, in a pup tent. One morning I got up and just keeled over and passed out.

I woke up in the hospital.

When something like that happens in the army, the standard operating procedure is for your superiors to secure your belongings, which they did, all of my belongings-- except my rifle, which disappeared.

When I got back to our barracks, my company commander, 1st Lt. Wasky, wanted to see me. He said that I was responsible for the loss of the rifle. He wanted me to sign a paper acknowledging that I would pay the $100 for its replacement.

I asked him, "Sir, since I passed out, how

can I be blamed for the rifle disappearing? Someone must have stolen it. Why wasn't an order immediately given to secure my rifle, just as my other equipment was?"

"Soldier," Lt. Wasky said, "when a paper is placed before you to sign in this man's army, you sign it, no questions asked."

"But sir—— " I started.

"Don't 'but sir' me, goddamn it," Lt. Wasky calmly replied.

"I'm going to make you my own personal project. I'm going to teach you how to sign a paper that's placed before you."

My life was miserable for the next four weeks until basic training was over. Lt. Wasky was personally on the hook with his superiors if a weapon went missing. So he did everything possible to force me to give in and sign the papers and pay for the replacement....

But I wouldn't do it!

(Now that looks nice in italics, don't you think?)

I got hit with every dirty detail you can imagine. When that didn't work, Lt. Wasky did things like have me driven in the middle of the night to some remote place on the base with me in full gear and I had to find my way back. What he was really hoping for was that I would take off and run AWOL, which would put me in the stockade.

Then on maneuvers, again Lt. Wasky called me into his tent with the drill sergeants present and verbally abused me, hoping that I would lose my cool and do something stupid.

"You really want to hit me," Lt. Wasky said. "Why don't you?"

There was only one small problem with that idea I thought: a 20-year sentence in Leavenworth! I just kept my hands to my sides and said as loud as I could, "No Sir!"

The drill sergeants poured it out also, right up to the last day when basic was over and we were given a two week leave before reporting to our next assignment for advanced training. For me, that was Ft. Knox, Kentucky. They made me stay doing menial tasks up until midnight when they had to let me go.

And then go I did, leaving 1st Lt. Wasky out $100 along with the much more expensive price of the embarrassment he experienced with his noncommissioned officers knowing that he could never break me. I never gave in, because I knew I was right. Sure, it would have been easy to sign the papers and have the money deducted from my pay, but the law within me that I've followed all my life would never let me do it, no matter what.

My hitch in the army served its purpose for me. When I got out, I went back home and attended New York University.

The four summer vacations that I had while attending New York University I spent playing with the ten piece dance band at Scaroon Manor in Schroon Lake, New York. It was located in the Adirondack Mountains half way between Lake George and the Canadian border. It catered to an upscale crowd looking to escape the frenzy of the Catskill resorts. We played in a band shell that looked like the Hollywood Bowl, outdoors in a huge amphitheater. It was a prestige job to land, not only because of the reputation it enjoyed, but it paid a musician more money than any other resort. One summer there they filmed *Marjorie Morningstar* starring Natalie Wood and Gene Kelly.

Because the guests were paying big bucks, management did not want any staff to mix with the single women guests and shut out the single men guests. However, I loved to dance to Latin music. So when the Latin band came on, alternating with our band, I would change my jacket in order not to be noticed and then I would ask one of the single guests to dance. This I did, of course, at the risk of being fired if I was caught. The director of *Marjorie Morningstar*, Irving Rappa, called me over and said, "I see what you're doing. You're a very good dancer." He put me in three scenes where ballroom dancing took place.

I almost got into a fist fight with Gene Kelly. One of the guests, Tina, a very sexy brunette, latched on to me. It was not unusual for girls to be attracted to musicians. First they went after the drummer of the band, then the jazz tenor sax player—- that was me. Kelly had big eyes for Tina, but she wouldn't give him the time of day. She would just wait for me to finish my gig, and then we hung out. You could see Kelly's ego was starting to take a slow burn. I'm sure he must've been wondering how she could turn down a big star like him for a band player. After what I observed at Performing Arts High School this display did not surprise me. One afternoon Kelly and I happened to be standing next to each other watching a ping pong match. Don't ask me what triggered it, but we started throwing garbs at each other which became real heated. I knew that I had better bite the bullet and walk away because no way I wouldn't be fired if this thing went any further.

I got a great education at NYU and eventually earned a Bachelor of Science degree in Marketing and Public Relations. One of my economic professors was Martin Gainsborough, head of the prestigious National Economic Council.

Besides my general course of studies, there were specific courses that I took that truly shaped and polished whatever business acumen I possessed before going to NYU. Alfred Gross, who taught the class of Sales and Salesmanship, actually wrote the textbook on that subject that was used by many business schools around the country. I'll never forget how one day walking into his classroom we observed on the entire blackboard what he explained was the baseball batting averages of different players. The lesson he pointed out was that the difference between a 300 batting average hitter who is considered a star and a 200 hitter who is considered mediocre is just one hit every third game. In other words, he was telling us how just a little extra effort to sell a prospective buyer can separate you from the herd. This lesson is what inspired me at William Morris never to look at the clock, unless I had an appointment, and to come in Saturdays and sometimes Sundays just to make that extra effort to be that 300 hitter.

Ironically, three elective courses made all

the difference in the world to me: Public Speaking where at the end of the course you had to give a 30 minute talk WITHOUT notes—- talk about honing your oratory skills; Business Writing, given by Mr. Janus who wrote the book on the subject, taught you how to draft a letter using language and key words regardless of grammatical correctness in order to drive your point home; and yes, Vocabulary Improvement was one of the most important courses I took. Why? Because it stressed that if you didn't know something, don't guess, look it up!

The girls in the NYU book store all had "the map of Ireland" on their faces. One of them asked if I was related to Cardinal Spellman. I said, "Yes, he's my uncle." Would you believe that I never paid for a book again?

Veterans attending the school were usually given a lot of latitude by our teachers. We would always sit in the back of a classroom together and give each other answers if we were stuck on a test. To this day, I'm still friendly with some of those guys.

I was really good at remembering the jokes I used to hear from all the comedians I saw in the resorts. So when the Student Service Organization would put on their annual show, I volunteered to be the Master of Ceremonies. If I do say so myself, I was really good at delivering the jokes and was a big hit, breaking the audiences up.

Even though my whole reason to get that degree was to immediately attract the job opportunities at the various theatrical agencies, I said to myself: I have been playing music since I was 8 years old, so how about one last fling as a musician before I enter the business world?

I took a job with the band at Grossinger's in the Catskills. How lucky for me! Unbeknownst to me, Milton Blackman kept an office at the hotel. Mr. Blackman was a power behind the scenes, discovering and molding future stars like Eddie Fisher. What he was doing working out of a Catskill resort two hours away from New York was beyond me, until I later found out that he was having an affair with Jenny Grossinger, the grand madam of the hotel.

I thought of approaching Mr. Blackman to solicit some career advice and maybe even a contact in showbiz. I figured that I had nothing to lose, and like a visiting lecturer at NYU admonished us, "Don't be afraid to walk into anyone's office and make your pitch. What's he going to do, bite your head off?"

So I knocked on Mr. Blackman's door.

"It's open," a voice said from inside.

I opened the door, and there Mr. Blackman sat behind a desk.

"Yes?" he asked.

"My name is Larry Spellman," I started, "and I work here at the hotel. I just got out of NYU and was wondering if you might spare a few moments to give me some career advice."

Mr. Blackman looked me up and down.

"Sure," he said. "Come on in and take a seat."

I came in and sat down.

"What kind of career?" Mr. Blackman

asked.

"Show business," I said.

"Actor?" Mr. Blackman asked.

"No," I said. "I want to be a theatrical agent."

"Oh?" Mr. Blackman asked, showing more interest.

"I have a Bachelor of Science in Marketing and Public Relations. I've spent years working as a professional musician and also in booking bands, my own and others."

"Why don't you pursue the music?" Mr. Blackman asked.

"Making deals happen is what I really want to do," I said.

Mr. Blackman smiled faintly.

"Know what you mean," Mr. Blackman said. "It's Larry, right?"

I nodded.

"So you want to become an agent," Mr. Blackman said.

"Not just any agent," I said. "I want to

handle stars, discover stars...make stars."

A twinkle lit in Mr. Blackman's eyes.

"Big talk," Mr. Blackman said.

"I'm thinking big," I said.

"Well," Mr. Blackman said, "it takes a while to make big thoughts turn into big things, but...."

Mr. Blackman looked me over.

"Saxophone," Mr. Blackman said.

"That's right," I said.

"I remember now," Mr. Blackman said. "I've seen you play. Well, if I was you, thinking big the way you're thinking now, I'd start right at the top. The very top. That would be the William Morris theatrical agency. They're the biggest and the best in the world. Think you're up to the biggest and best?"

"I know I am," I said.

"You need to contact Nat Lefkowitz," Mr. Blackman said. "He's the head of the New York William Morris office."

"How would I contact him?" I asked.

Mr. Blackman studied me again.

"I'll write you a letter of recommendation to him," Mr. Blackman said. "That'll get you in."

"Thank you, Mr. Blackman," I said.

"Don't mention it," Mr. Blackman replied.

Mr. Blackman's letter of recommendation got me an interview with the personnel director at William Morris, a guy who I only remember now as Ray something or other. After my interview with Ray, he sent me up to the comptroller's office who oversaw the personnel director. Sid Feinberg was the comptroller's name. I remember him because he chatted a lot about his art collection. Then Feinberg got off his art and got on to the subject of me.

"I see you graduated from NYU in June," Feinberg said.

"That's right," I said.

"It's now November," Feinberg said. "Why have you waited so long to apply for our training program?"

I said, "I've been playing music since I was

eight years old and I've been a professional union musician since high school. When I graduated in June I just wanted one, last fling as a musician before I put down the horns. And since I got an offer to join the band at Grossinger's up in the Catskills, I just couldn't turn it down. And that's what I've been doing since June, playing in the band up at Grossinger's."

"I see," Feinberg said.

"That's how I made the acquaintance of Mr. Blackman, who gave me the letter of recommendation."

"He was up at Grossinger's?" Feinberg asked.

"He has an office there," I said.

"Really," Feinberg said. "How did you get in to see him?"

"I knocked on his door," I replied.

Feinberg looked me in the eye. It had the same quality of a "click" when the last number on a combination lock is spun into place.

"All right," Feinberg said. "That'll be all for

now. We'll give you a call."

I went out of Feinberg's office fairly certain I had the job.

And then a week later on the first Thursday in November '59, when I wasn't expecting it, I got the call that Feinberg had promised. The call came early morning in the morning. I was still in bed as I was out late the night before. The guy on the line was Ray, the personnel director at William Morris.

"When can you start?" Ray asked.

"How about tomorrow?" I asked.

"Monday will be fine," Ray said.

Do I have to tell you how flying high I was all weekend long? I had made it on the first rung of my career plan, a very high rung, I thought.

But then it didn't seem so high when I stood there in the rain with those kinescopes gripped in my hand that Monday morning of my first day on the job.

The rain was pouring down in sheets...the sidewalk laying ahead of me on Madison Avenue seemed to stretch away to infinity...and that advertising agency...just where the hell was that advertising agency, anyway...?

CHAPTER THREE

Law on the Fast Track

Well, I did locate that advertising agency on Madison Avenue. And I did manage to put myself back together in some kind of presentable condition before returning to the William Morris offices. Actually, after that first day, things went very smoothly on my job. I started performing the men's room gig every morning without even thinking about it. The mailroom work was routine. It demanded my time and my physical focus, but not my brain.

While I was working in the mail room, my mother had a heart attack and died. Heart disease was very common among Jewish people in those days. They ate a lot of fatty foods, heavy meats. My mother used to put a whole salt shaker on her food. Nobody really understood how bad this kind of thing was back then. You never heard the word "cholesterol." Everybody just ate, and you ate everything. Plus, everybody worked very hard. All this was sure to shorten a life span. After my mother's death, I continued to live in our Bronx apartment. Now my focus became entirely my work.

Of course the mailroom job at William Morris was just an entry level position. Everybody at the agency started out there, unless you were an established agent hired away from one of the other major agencies. Few trainees at William Morris stayed in the mail room very long. Usually it was either up or out. But although I was doing very well on my job, after 14 months, I was still there doing it, while other guys in the mailroom had already moved up to the position of secretary to an agent, the next rung in the William Morris ladder. I stagnated in the mailroom job, not because there weren't any openings for secretarial jobs on the next level, but because I was holding out for what I considered the plum job of the next level of jobs: secretary to Nat Kalcheim, Senior Administrator to *all the other agents*, and one of the founding fathers of the agency itself.

Even though it was a gamble on my part turning down offers to become a secretary and get out of the mailroom sooner, I knew that if I could land Kalcheim's spot and hopefully impress him that I would eventually move up the ladder faster with him behind me. I never expected that it would take 14 months in the mailroom for that opening to happen.

As it turned out, the gamble paid off.

Kalcheim's secretary finally moved up the ladder, and I grabbed the opportunity.

I lost 15 pounds working for Kalcheim. He was an inveterate letter and memo writer. Even though while in the mailroom we went to a secretarial school to learn shorthand and typing (fortunately I took a year of typing in high school), I wasn't the greatest secretary in the world. In order to finish all his work, I never took a lunch hour. I would come in Saturdays and some Sundays, so that, when he came into the office on Monday morning, his letters were waiting for his signature.

I knew he appreciated the effort I was making to please him, especially when he heard from Sid Berkowitz, one of the accountants in the office. Berkowitz said that one Sunday, when he happened to come into the office, he saw me typing away while I was wearing my tuxedo. Don't forget that I was still working gigs as a musician on the weekends and would go to the office before and sometimes in between jobs. I knew that Berkowitz mentioned this to Kalcheim.

One Sunday I didn't have a music job but wanted to go into the office and finish up Kalcheim's dictation. Nobody was ever in the office on Sundays. Berkowitz's appearance that one time was unusual. So on this Sunday I brought my Doberman Pinscher Rusty with me and let her roam while I was working.

Suddenly, I heard a SCREAM from around the other end of the corridor.

It scared the heck out of me. I went running to see what was wrong.

Don Kopaloff, one of the motion picture

agents, was pinned against the wall of his office.

Rusty was just staring at Don.

Who would ever expect to be scared witless when going to the office on a nice, quiet Sunday-- and I really think on that Sunday Don really *did* scare Rusty witless.

You see, Rusty was not only a Doberman, but also a big, fat *pussy cat.*

But working as a professional musician and a full-time secretary was a complicated shuffle for me. I had to keep working as a musician to make ends meet because my secretarial job paid so little. My drive and commitment impressed Mr. Kalcheim, but I really won him over on one of those working Saturdays when I performed a little magic all my own.

The phone rang, and I picked it up.

"Mr. Kalcheim's office," I answered.

The man on the other end had a voice that sounded like it belonged to somebody important. If the man had been a musical instrument—- say a violin—- he would have been a Stradivarius. But

78

right now, he was a Stradivarius in need of tuning. Something was wrong. This was a man who was not used to being flustered. And as is always the case in such situations, he was having some difficulty in clearly expressing his thoughts.

"I'm sorry," I said. "I just didn't quite understand what you were saying. Could you please repeat it?"

"Look," the man said, "it's a disaster. This event is very important."

"Where did you say you were calling from?" I asked.

"Right over here at the UN!" the man snapped. "I'm personal friends with Nat Kalcheim."

That got my instant attention.

"Yes, sir," I said. "Mr. Kalcheim is not in today, but I'm his personal secretary. Perhaps I can help you."

"I have a crowd of children over here who are going to be very disappointed if something isn't done," the man said in true desperation. "The magician we hired to perform for them has called in sick. Can you supply us with another magician?"

My brain clicked. Where in the world could I find a magician?

"We need him to be here in less than an hour," the man added, almost seeming to go out of breath.

My brain clicked again. Where in the world could I find a magician in less than an hour?

"Sir," I said, going on a kind of automatic pilot, "please give me your number and I will call you back almost immediately."

The man gave me his number and he hung up.

I had to get the man off the line so that I could concentrate. As soon as I hung up, I looked about the room, thinking: magician, magician, magician. Where would I look myself if I needed a magician to do a show in less than an hour? My eye fell on a New York City telephone directory on a shelf under a table. I grabbed the directory, flipped through it to the Yellow Pages, looked under

Magicians, and dialed the first listing my eyes fell upon.

A man answered and identified himself by some magician's stage name I no longer remember. Let's call him the Great How-are-you.

"How-are-you?" I asked.

"Yes," he said (so that *had* to be his name), "I'm fine. How are you?"

"Very good," I said. "I'm Larry Spellman with the William Morris Agency."

"Is this a gag?" the Great How-are-you asked.

"No gag," I said. "This is really the William Morris Agency. I have a client with an emergency over at the UN. His magician just called in sick for a kid's show, and he needs a fill-in act."

"Wait," the Great How-are-you asked, "you're telling me that you really *are* the William Morris Agency?"

"Yes," I said, "I'm really with WMA."

"WMA!" the Great How-are-you exclaimed. "You *are* legit! You know the lingo! I can't believe it! William Morris! After all these years! Finally! Finally! I have been...*discovered!* Mabel! Mabel, come in here! It's William Morris calling! For me! For *me*!"

It sounded like the Great How-are-you was almost in tears.

"Hey, hey," I said. "It's just a kid's show! A fill-in!"

"How—- how did you find me?" the Great How-are-you asked. "It was the show at the Shriners, wasn't it? It *had* to be! Thank God I had the presence of mind to bring along the Astra Levitation! Not that cheap Zombie Ball! You couldn't see the mechanism, could you? Could you? I tell you, I'm ready for Sullivan!"

"This is just a fill-in job," I said. "Do you want it or not?"

"Oh, I get it!" the Great How-are-you said. "This is a *test*—- an audition! You're screening talent for Sullivan! I get it! I get it! Of course I want the job! When is it?"

"In less than an hour," I said. "Can you

82

make it?"

"To the UN?" the Great How-are-you asked. "A kid's show?"

"A kid's show," I said. "*Not* Ed Sullivan."

"I can make it," the Great How-are-you said. "My assistant and I are on our way! Mabel! Mabel! Get dressed! I got a job!"

"Just hold it right where you are," I said. "I have to call the client back and confirm the booking. Then I'll call you back and give you directions. And one other thing."

"Yes?" the Great How-are-you asked.

"Don't bring that Astra thing," I said. "Just bring some tricks. And a rabbit, if you have one."

I hung up and called the man at the UN back with the good news. He was overjoyed, and suddenly sounded like a perfectly tuned Stradivarius. I called the Great How-are-you back and gave him some specific directions. By now, reality had sunk in on him and he wanted to know how much he was going to get paid.

"Scale," I said.

"Scale?" the Great How-are-you asked. "How much is scale?"

"I'll get back to you on that," I said, and hung up.

Well, the kid's magic show at the UN turned out to be a big hit. I even learned that the Great How-are-you in fact *did* have a white rabbit that he pulled out of his hat. And *I* in booking the magician out of the Yellow Pages had pulled a rabbit out of *my* hat. The guy from the United Nations very graciously called Mr. Kalcheim and expressed his gratitude, and that impressed Mr. Kalcheim.

"How did you get the magician so quick?" Mr. Kalcheim asked me.

"I just used the Yellow Pages," I said.

Mr. Kalcheim threw his head back and laughed.

One of the thrills of working for a man of Kalcheim's stature was meeting big stars like Sammy Davis, Jr. who came into the office. Kalcheim would also encourage me to listen in on his phone calls which would not only help me learn things by osmosis, but be more aware of what he was doing.

I jumped out of my seat one day when I answered the phone in the usual manner, "Mr. Kalcheim's office," and found that it was Frank Sinatra calling. He was calling to ask Mr. Kalcheim to join him for the Kennedy inauguration in Washington.

One day I was in the men's room and at the next urinal was Sid Feinberg, remember? The comptroller?

Feinberg just casually blurted out, "Do you know you are being discussed by the administration about your outside booking of music acts?"

I was really taken aback by this because I could see where this could lead to my dismissal if it went any further.

I ran into Kalcheim's office and told him what just took place.

I said to him, "I cannot believe that the William Morris Agency that represents some of the biggest stars in the world is going to consider me booking weddings and bar mitzvahs on weekends as competition. And there's no way I can support myself on my salary here of sixty-five dollars a week. I need that one hundred to one hundred-fifty dollars I'm making on weekends to survive."

Mr Kalcheim said, "Don't worry. I'll take care of it."

And he did.

This is another example of why spending 14 months in the mailroom was worth it. Having Mr. Kalcheim in your corner throughout your life at the office made your position much stronger.

A final event sealed Mr. Kalcheim's belief in me: In those days the big hotels all had famous house bands, like Guy Lombardo at the Roosevelt Hotel in Manhattan and Freddy Martin at the Ambassador Hotel in Los Angeles. When Freddy Martin decided to leave the Ambassador, it was announced to Mr. Kalcheim while I was taking his dictation. He was discussing possible replacements with another agent and not having much success.

Suddenly, I blurted out, "I have the perfect

replacement!"

Mr. Kalcheim and the other agent stared at me.

"Sorry," I said. "I didn't mean to interrupt."

"No," Mr. Kalcheim said, "tell us. Who do you think would be the perfect replacement?"

I said, "We should replace Freddy Martin with the Swing and Sway of Sammy Kaye!"

Mr. Kalcheim looked at the other agent who nodded slowly, and then he looked back at me.

"It's a natural," Mr. Kalcheim said. "Sammy Kaye. That's the answer. We'll do it!" Mr. Kalcheim leaped on to my idea, and, in one symbolic gesture, took me under his wing, making me an assistant agent. I first was made an assistant agent for George Kane and then Steve Jacobs who was Kalcheim's secretary before me.

As an assistant I would still function as a secretary to the full agent (Jacobs) but now I started to handle marginal, nightclub accounts. This is where I started to make a name for myself.

In New York City in those days every

borough, as well as Long Island, New Jersey and Connecticut had nightclubs that played talent on the weekends. We had a lot of performers on the list who were either hot at one time, but no longer, or were up-and-coming artists. It was the possibility of booking these venues that kept these performers alive while they were waiting for the next big break in their careers. I really put my nose to the grindstone and relentlessly went after these accounts and was able to make a lot of bookings for the artists of this type on our roster. I used to wonder why a major agency such as ours would bother to get jobs for performers like this, but then, after I got into the business of the nightclubs, I understood why. It would sometimes take six months for one of our TV series packaging agents to sell a series to a network or a sponsor, or for a motion picture agent to finalize an important deal. What paid the electric bill meanwhile? Nightclub and concert bookings.

Where I really created some noise about myself was when one of our senior nightclub agents, Sam Bramson, an icon in the agency world, booked a singing act that had just formed. It was Dick Haymes who had made major recordings and had done movies and his new wife Fran Jeffries, one of the sexiest, most talked-about ladies of that time. They were set to open in New York at one of the premier clubs in Manhattan, The Round Table. It was a much anticipated opening amongst the jet setters. What they were dying to do first was find a club where they could break in the act. None of the agents could come up with it. Bramson and Paul Cantor, the agent who had signed the act to the office, were getting desperate. Guess who came up with the booking? I found a little weekend place on Route 46 in New Jersey, twenty miles from the Lincoln Tunnel. I talked the owner into what a coup this would be for him if he would just stretch his budget this one time. Haymes himself couldn't stop thanking me, which was nice, let alone all the points I made with Bramson and Kalcheim.

Finding clubs like this that the office didn't know existed or just didn't want to bother with, and developing them into active, flourishing accounts got my name around William Morris in a big way-- especially when Jane Russell decided that she wanted to do a singing act because nothing was happening for her in the movies anymore. Again, I came up with the break-in dates that she needed. The first date was really a place no one knew existed, Uncle Miltie's in Camden, New Jersey. All the guys asked me, "How did you come up with that one?"

Because of this buzz about me, Roz Ross sought me out when she joined the office. At that time, Rock and Roll became popular enough for William Morris to want to be a part of it. They started their own Rock department by hiring Roz Ross, an agent at one of our competitors, General Artists Corp. Roz brought her full stall of artists: Paul Anka, Bobby Rydell, Fabian, Gene Pitney, and others. She took me under her wing and encouraged me to sign new artists, inspiring in me an even more aggressive style. What I gleaned from my working relationship with her served me well. Her focus was always on signing the act for representation, thereby providing the agency with a roster of artists that covered a wider range. My first try at her technique resulted in signing *Paul and Paula*, who had the No. 1 record at that time. I learned that it was just as easy to sell the act on the agency as it was to sell the act to the buyers. Roz convinced my superiors that I had executive potential. She named me "Mr. Tenacity." It stuck. That was when I realized that I could sell anyone to anyone.

I was elevated to full agent when I joined Roz Ross, but I had no secretary of my own just yet, so I did all of my own typing. The fun part was sharing an office with the great and hilarious Wally Amos who later founded the Famous Amos chain of cookie shops.

I would go with Wally to places like the Apollo Theater in Harlem where we would cover the black groups who were hot in those days. The Ronettes, the Exciters, Big Dee Irwin and Ruby & the Romantics were just some of them.

An event that occurred with Wally that I'll never forget was when I was booking an Arlo Guthrie-type folk-music room in Greenwich Village. Those days the Kingston Trio, the Weavers, the Limelighters, Jessie Colin Young and the group Peter, Paul & Mary were the hot acts with the college crowds. Wally asked me to get a job in this folk-music club for a new act that he had just signed to William Morris named Simon & Garfunkel. He said for me to get them any kind of money, even a $125 a week, just to get them started. I said, "Wally, what kind of name is Simon & Garfunkel? That's not a showbiz name. Tell them to change their name." Of course, Wally didn't do that. I made the booking anyway.

And the rest is showbiz history.

This illustrates that there are no guaranteed formulae in the business of showbiz; it's not a science, it's an art, and a very unpredictable art at that!

A personal learning experience about marriage came to me from Wally Amos one day. Wally was only 27 years old at that time, and was already married with kids. Sharing an office, it was hard to have secrets from each other. I knew he had a steady girlfriend on the side.

I said, "You know, Wally, with that girlfriend, you're playing with fire."

"It's not getting caught cheating that will hurt you," Wally replied. "What'll *kill* you are those *two dinners* you have to eat seven nights a week!"

Owch! Wally Amos was fun and funny and I loved working with him.

Roz Ross really drove us hard. One-nighter tours were common in the Rock and Roll world. First of all, when booking a tour you had to get bookings that followed each other in a logistical way to accommodate acceptable travel time. To make a tour economically sound, you would need at least 5 days out of the 7 booked, again in a perfect route. If one of the engagements fell out for one reason or another, the entire tour could be in trouble financially. God forbid that you left the office before 9 or 10 pm if you didn't replace that date.

While I was functioning in the Rock department headed by Roz Ross, Kalcheim still wanted me to be attached simultaneously to the nightclub department because of the relationships I had built up with my accounts and because the office still cared about those artists for whom I had gotten all that work. This all dovetailed nicely, because eventually Roz wanted to move some of the Rock and Roll names like Bobby Rydell and Paul Anka up to the nightclub world where they could start building an older audience. I was able to make those transitions for her because of the relationships I had with the club owners.

One of the great commentaries about how subjective show business is and how nobody wrote the book on what can or cannot happen in that business was evidenced by an episode that took place between Roz Ross and Steve Blauner, Bobby Darin's manager.

Bobby Darin was hot as a pistol in the Rock and Roll world because of his smash hit record

Splish Splash I Was Taking A Bath. Blauner came in to see Roz Ross and told her of his idea about recording Darin in a "swing" version of Louis Armstrong's hit *Mack the Knife*.

You could hear Roz screaming at the top of her lungs, "You're crazy! You're going to ruin this kid!"

Again, of course, the rest is showbiz history.

Don't forget that Roz Ross was considered the grand madam of the music industry. It was a valuable lesson that all of show business is actually "a law unto itself." There are no set rules, never have been, never will be.

I finally got a secretary when Roz asked me to move in with Sherman Tankel, my first mailroom boss. Sherman had now made a name for himself in Roz's department booking strictly the college market. Colleges all over the country were playing attractions on their campuses and paying big money. Sherman got so busy booking the Smothers Brothers, Bill Cosby, the Lettermen and many other attractions that were hot on the circuit that he needed help if he was going to expand. Roz asked me to join him and the two of us with our own secretary, Jay Jacobs, really opened up that market in a big way.

In those days acts would show their appreciation for what an agent did for them all year long by showering them with expensive gifts at Christmas. Sherman got some really beautiful and expensive gifts from all the acts on his college roster. But the act that made the most money that year was the Smothers Brothers. Sherman couldn't wait to see what they were going to get for him!

Sherman sat there, big and stout, with his now *three* double chins, opening gift after gift. His Christmas spirit was so high he was starting to run a fever.

"Sherman! Sherman!" I kept saying. "Open the one from the Smother's Brothers!"

And Sherman kept replying, "No, no! The Smothers gift is the cream on the cake! The cherry on the sundae! The gold in the goldie-lox!"

Finally, Sherman had torn through every

gift, wrapping paper everywhere, gifts everywhere, expensive watches, gold-inlaid pen sets, and-- can-you-believe-it, season tickets to the Yankees?

"Now," Sherman said, his Christmas-fever practically breaking into a sweat, "the Smothers Brothers! It's going to be a biggie!"

Sherman reached across his desk to a large, flat box. He got hold of it with both hands and started ferociously tearing at it. He stepped over and grabbed a letter opener, and then I could only see his back and his elbows working frantically, his head bobbing, his body practically shaking. Sherman was having...a Christmas...epiphany.

Suddenly, Sherman's head went back, and he SCREAMED.

"No!"   Sherman   wailed. "Nooo...ho...ho...ho!"

I couldn't help it—- I thought of Santa Claus.

"No," Sherman cried, "they can't do this to me!"

Sherman slowly turned around, and I saw all

three of his double chins quivering back and forth, and clutched tightly in his hands, the present that the Smothers Brothers had sent him.

It was a calendar of themselves.

That was it.

Really.

Sherman and Roz had an acrimonious relationship and Sherman left to join a hot new start-up agency, Chartwell Artists who had the Righteous Brothers, Mamas & the Papas, and the Christy Minstrels. I inherited the whole college business which I didn't want as I didn't want to be pigeonholed. I liked the diversity of the bookings I was doing, Rock and Roll, one-nighters, nightclubs, some colleges, and I started making record deals, selling artists to record companies, and most importantly, signing acts of a diverse nature.

I held down the fort until the office brought in Steve Leber who ran his own college booking agency in Boston and was a specialist in that area. Eventually Roz Ross burned out and moved to Arizona. After that, Steve became the head of the entire one-nighter department and built it into a big success. He eventually left William Morris with another member of his department, Dave Krebs, when they got the rights to book the concert tour of *Jesus Christ Superstar*. They also went on to produce the Broadway show *Beatlemania.*

While still at the office, Dave Krebs brought me in to help him sign Brook Benton to William Morris. Benton was real hot at the time with the hit record *A Rainy Night in Georgia*. The three of us went to lunch at the Warwick Hotel around the corner from the office. I went into my whole shpill during the entire luncheon as to why Benton would be well served if he signed with the William Morris Agency. And he did sign.

When Dave Krebs got back to the office he said to Lee Stevens, the number two head of the New York office: "After hearing Larry Spellman talk, *I* wanted to sign with William Morris!"

CHAPTER FOUR

Law of Attraction

In the early 1960s the hottest dance craze was the Twist. Joey Dee & the Starliters and Chubby Checker were the two hottest bands in the country playing this music. The Peppermint Lounge on 46th Street off Broadway in Manhattan was the place to be seen. U.S. Senator Jake Javitz from New York was always there twisting the night away, as well as movie stars and other celebrities.

Having been inspired by my boss Roz Ross to be aggressive about signing new artists to the office, I started to wage a campaign to try to sign Joey Dee to William Morris.

I learned that Dee's agency papers were about to expire with his current agent Jolly Joyce who was out of Philadelphia.

Dee kept an office in Manhattan, and I would go over there periodically, "romancing" him. Here I learned a valuable lesson from this experience that would stay with me the rest of my professional life.

One afternoon when I went to see Dee, Jolly Joyce was there, trying to re-sign Joey to his agency. Joyce, of course, knew why I was there and made a point of engaging me in "friendly" conversation.

At one point Joyce said, "Larry, off the record, just between you and me, do you think Joey is going to go with you over to William Morris?"

I innocently answered, "It's a good possibility."

Next thing I knew, a few days later I get called into Joe Singer's office. Singer was a brilliant lawyer and head of business affairs for William Morris. Singer said that I was being brought up on charges by the American Guild of Variety Artists because I had been trying to sign Joey Dee to WMA. Apparently there was a rule that an agent could not solicit an act's representation while the act was still signed to another agent; you had to wait until the act's authorization papers expired, and then you could pursue. Joey Dee was still being represented by Jolly Joyce, so my discussions with Joey Dee had violated WMA's agreement with AGVA. Fortunately, Joe Singer was highly respected. The hearing he and I attended at the Guild's office ended with me just receiving a reprimand, being that I was a relatively new agent. Sol Shapiro, number two head of the WMA Personal Appearance Department, drove home to me the lesson I had learned when he said to me: "There is no such thing as 'off the record'!"

I backed off pursuing Joey Dee & the Starliters. But one good thing came out of all this. I got to meet Gloria, Joey's secretary, a double for Elizabeth Taylor. Gloria was recently divorced from Bill Shoemaker, the famous jockey.

After one or two dates with Gloria, she said to me: "I really think that you and my girlfriend Anna would be right for each other...."

And we were!

Anna and I hit it off right away and were hot

and heavy for the next year and a half.

Anna was eloquently beautiful. She came to New York from San Diego as a model. When I met her, she was running the showroom for Christian Dior.

One time, Lee Salomon, a senior night club agent at WMA, wanted to make a showing at the Town & Country nightclub in Brooklyn where Tony Bennett was headlining. Salomon was trying to sign him to the office. He invited a group of us in order to show Bennett how interested the agency was in him. Naturally, I brought Anna as my date. When Lee saw her, his mouth opened up with amazement.

I wasn't surprised by Lee's reaction to Anna. Her beauty *was* amazing. And the fact that she was with me was also amazing. What she saw in me was a mystery. Here I was, a guy with no discernible style, not particularly sophisticated, and she had her pick of many wealthy, successful bachelors. Go figure. We were madly in love.

Anna took me shopping for my first real

wardrobe. My father had been a tailor, but I had never given all that much thought to my clothing. Anna explained suits to me, how they were put together, how a coat should fit around the neck and shoulders. She knew fabrics and colors and everything about fashion for both men and women. She had an artist's eye—- and a woman's touch. Incredible to say, but I hadn't known what I had been missing. I had never been a slob, but suddenly, I realized, Anna was turning me into a...*gentleman*.

Anna not only dressed me, but taught me how to make love to a woman who needed to be satisfied. She was patient, and gentle, and (c'mon guys!)...*kind*. She taught me not to rush, to take my time. *She* definitely was not in a hurry. Like one night when we were in bed, in the middle of a heavy sexual experience. I was just about to have an orgasm, when she just suddenly pushed me off of her, jumped out of bed, ran to the window, and yelled:

"Snow! Snow!"

I couldn't believe what was happening. Anna had grown up in San Diego and had never seen snow before, and her first sight of it was overwhelming to her, even more than sex.

Then Anna coaxed me out of my Bronx apartment and into my first place in Manhattan. It was in a brand new building at 310 west 56th Street, off Eighth Avenue. It was just two blocks from the office, and it had a doorman! The apartment was an L-shaped studio, technically a one bedroom, just no wall separating the bed from the living room. My hands shook when I signed the $180 per month lease. I totally furnished the apartment on credit from Gimbel's department store, right across the street from Macy's, their direct competitors.

I was in my Manhattan apartment only a few months when my 27th birthday rolled around on June 20th, 1963. Things were starting to really look up. I was making real progress at the office. Besides my salary finally becoming respectable, the office was giving me perks like paying for the garage where I parked my convertible and my car insurance. I had an expense account and was going out at least five nights a week, seeing shows at nightclubs all over New York.

At that same time, Mel Marx, who was the brother of my NYU buddy Harvey, became good friends with me because Harvey decided to get married. Mel introduced me to Marv Gold and Sam Ravitz. Ironically, Sam also lived on Fulton Avenue in the Bronx when he was 3 to 5 years old. I didn't know him then, but apparently my brothers were friends with his brothers...small world. Well, the four of us really hit it off and started to have a lot of fun together as bachelors. It stayed that way for a solid four years until we all got married, and married we all got—- and all in the same year! Once one of us dropped out, the others didn't want to be the last man out. Crazy, isn't it?

Unfortunately, this taste of success at William Morris coupled with my new-found bachelor experience caused my break-up with Anna. Don't forget that I worked as a musician every weekend throughout school, not dating like the other guys. My early days at the office were work and no money, working weekends again. Now that things were going my way, I just wanted to finally enjoy life without being tied down to a wife and kids. I knew that Anna wanted to get married.

That summer of 1963 I decided to use my two week vacation to travel to Europe for my very first time—- ALONE—- and think things over. Anna actually helped me pack and my brother Jerry drove me to JFK airport. There, I boarded an Air France flight to Paris. In Paris, I wandered through the streets, absorbing every detail of the most beautiful city I had ever seen.

One night atop the Eiffel Tower, I looked out upon the shimmering City of Lights and realized with certain suddenness that I wanted to move on with my life. I knew I loved Anna, had loved her passionately, madly, but, as much as I felt for her, I knew it was not enough. Something was missing. I could have gone on, pretending, but it would have been wrong, wrong for both of us. The law within me spoke, quietly, firmly, finally, while the lights of Paris continued to shimmer.

When I got back home, I called her and broke it off. I cried for three months straight, and then got on with my life. Anna left her job and moved to San Francisco just to get away and start anew.

And I was starting life anew myself. Things were about to happen that I would have never believed a short while earlier. And to just give you a hint...I was about to build the career of Jimmy Roselli, a singer with a big hit record—- backed by the mob!

CHAPTER FIVE

Law and Disorder

I was still dating Anna when I went to see Jimmy Roselli perform for the first time.

Jimmy Roselli, a singer from Hoboken, New Jersey, was a childhood friend of Frank Sinatra's. Roselli sang around the local clubs, impressing nobody. But then he cut a record called *Mala Femina* ("Bad Woman"), sung in Italian. Jack O'Brien, a famous disk jockey on WMCA, broke the record and made Jimmy hot.

At our office, Lee Salomon got a call from a friend of Roselli's, informing him that Roselli was going to perform at the 802 Club in Brooklyn. The friend asked Salomon to send someone from our office to see Roselli. I never found out who this friend was, but he was probably one of the Mafia guys who were backing Roselli, maybe even a guy I came to know as "Buckalo," a guy I will tell more about later.   Salomon told me to go check out Roselli.

The 802 Club was a local, mob-run nightclub, nothing glamorous or ostentatious about it.   It was somewhat cavernous inside and held about three or four hundred people.   Charlie Rusinak, who was the owner, ran the place.   There was no maître d'.   Charlie sat you down.   They served simple Italian dinners: spaghetti and meatballs and for desert spumoni.

When we arrived at the club, I saw its neon sign overhead and crowds of people moving toward its double doors.   We went in with the others, found Charlie Rusinak, and I introduced myself to him.

"Been expecting you," Charlie said.   "Where do you want to sit?

"In the back," I said.

"I can put you up front," Charlie said.

"I prefer the back," I said.

Charlie led me through the crowd to a table at the back of the hall.   I wanted to watch not only Roselli, but the crowd and their reactions.   The audience was 99% Italian, ranging in age from the late 20s to the early 50s. The men all wore suits and ties. The women all wore tight cocktail dresses with low-cut necklines showing plenty of cleavage and breast. I watched these people with detachment, but made note of a certain excitement in the air that I had previously only encountered before the performance of a big name star.

The dinner they served was passable, but Charlie Rusinak came by me a couple of times, and asked, "Everything—- it's a okay?"

"Fine, fine," I said.

"Jimmy's just about ready," Rusinak said. "He's coming out—- soon as desert!"

Rusinak disappeared once again. I kept watching the people. Their excitement was growing. I could especially hear it in the voices of the women. The laughter of women's voices kept erupting in the club.

Suddenly there was a hush, as if someone had given an unseen cue—- the band struck a chord—- and Jimmy Roselli came bounding up on to the stage amid a tidal wave of applause. I pushed my desert plate aside, and focused on Roselli.

He was short and stocky, and although he was dressed in a dark suit and tie, he looked like a truck driver. But the moment he opened his mouth to sing, he was transformed into something else entirely. He became a powerhouse of emotion, an interpreter of destiny——- a star.

From the moment that Roselli started singing, it was obvious that he held that crowd in the palm of his hand.

After the show, Charlie Rusinak led Anna and me back to the dressing room and introduced us to Roselli.

"Thanks for coming," Roselli said.

"Loved your show," I said. "It knocked me out."

"So you think I've got something?" Roselli asked.

"Oh," I said, "you've got something, all right. I'd sign you right now, but my bosses are on the conservative side. They don't want me to move too fast. It would be good if I could see you perform again somewhere."

Roselli said, "If you want to see me really perform, come next Saturday. I'm booked up in the Bronx at the Chateau Pelham."

I said, "I'll make it a point to come see you."

The Chateau Pelham was in the Parkway section of the northeast Bronx, right under the elevated trains. It was a big, one-story catering hall owned by Tony Amendola. Across the street from the Chateau Pelham was a restaurant named Amen's which would figure significantly in my life in the coming months.

Unlike the Club 802, the Chateau Pelham had an air of elegance. The tables there were covered in white linen tablecloths and were set in a horseshoe configuration around a makeshift stage. The place, which held about 2,000 people, usually booked weddings. It had now been transformed into a nightclub for Roselli's performance.

The night I went to see Roselli at Chateau

Pelham two other couples joined Anna and me. The first couple was Stan Rubin and his wife. Stan played clarinet and was the leader of the Tiger Town Five, the Dixieland band that Grace Kelly flew to Monaco for her wedding. The other couple was Enrico (he just went by the one name) and his girlfriend Greta, a tall gorgeous showgirl who was a regular on the Jackie Gleason TV show. Enrico was a very handsome singer from Italy that Johnny Carson had on his show many times. Enrico moved in mob circles. On one of my vacations from William Morris, I flew to Miami and stayed with Enrico at his friend's retreat. The friend was Mike Chima, one of the biggest bosses in Pittsburgh. I ate enough lasagna that week to last me a lifetime!

The night we went to Chateau Pelham, the six of us—- Stan, his wife, Enrico, Greta, Anna and me—- were in the car together. Just as we turned and pulled up underneath the elevator trains to park, I couldn't believe my eyes.

Busloads—- *busloads* of people pulling up in groups!

"Is Roselli this hot?" I asked.

We all got out of the car and went in. Roselli had made a reservation for us and the maître d' took us to our table, which was about one row back from ringside. The place was packed.

Just as we got seated, Enrico's face lit up as he looked about the room.

"Oh, my God," Enrico said. "Look who's here. Some of the biggest boys are here!"

Enrico nodded to his right and left. I looked and saw several Italian men dressed in dark suits and ties. They looked like accountants, but I knew by Enrico calling them "boys" that they were the mob.

We all had dinner, and, once again, I felt the electricity in the audience. There was a definite feeling that something big was about to happen.

As desert was served, again that hush sounded, and this time the wave of quiet seemed to roll toward us from the back of the hall. The band struck its chord—-

And there was Jimmy Roselli.

116

The crowd went wild with applause. Here, he wasn't the Star; he was family, the gifted brother, the shining pride of two thousand.

The applause continued. Roselli raised the microphone in his hand and smiled. He had us all.

Then Roselli went into his first song. He sang a lot of popular songs, a lot of standards, and he interspersed among them a lot of Italian songs. It was his own interpretation of the Italian songs that made him different from other Italian singers. His singing style was almost operatic. That is, he had the kind of power in his voice that opera singers have. He could hold a high note for the longest time. He delivered his songs with a lot of heart. It was so reminiscent to me of what I used to hear growing up going to Jewish synagogues. Roselli's singing style was what I would call "cantorial," a style I later learned was somewhat indigenous to Neopolitan singers. They all sing in that same—- what I call—- "cantorial" mode.

Roselli just had that ability to "wow" an audience, something I have called the "x factor."

You can't teach it. You either have it or you don't. Roselli had it. He killed that audience. Roselli was reminiscent to me of Al Jolson, a guy who could get down on one knee and kill an audience. Roselli electrified that audience. He electrified *me*. I really loved the way he sang.

Roselli sang a good hour and twenty minutes. When he finished his show, the audience leapt to its feet, applauding—-
and they kept applauding. They didn't want to let him go. I was astounded.

When Roselli finally got off, I made my way back to his dressing room which was just the room where the brides would change. As soon as I got back there, Roselli was waiting for me. I think he knew I wanted to sign him. It wasn't just the look on my face. After a performance like that, an agent would have had to have been crazy not to sign him—- and he knew it.

"I'm in," Roselli said to me.

I shook his hand.

"Can you come to the office on Monday and

sign the paperwork?" I asked.

"I think I can arrange to be there," Roselli said, grinning.

I was just as excited as Roselli. Really, I was just starting out, just like Roselli, and I was prepared to take us all the way to the top.

Roselli came into the office and signed a standard WMA contract under the aegis of the American Guild of Variety Artists. Following this, Roselli and I had an initial discussion about the strategy of his career.

"You need to meet a friend of mine," Roselli said. "He's taken a personal interest in me and given me great advice. I wouldn't be here right now, signed with William Morris, if it wasn't for him."

"What's his name?" I asked.

"Buckalo," Roselli said.

"Buckalo?" I asked. "Is that his first or last name?"

"That's *all* of his name," Roselli said. "He

just goes by Buckalo. Don't ask him for more. He doesn't like that."

"I get it," I said. "Well, where do I find Buckalo?"

Roselli directed me to Amen's, that restaurant in the northeast Bronx I mentioned earlier, right across the street from Chateau Pelham. Tony Amendola's nephew, Charlie Amen, ran Amen's. I used to love to go there because the food was so good. Buckalo held court there at Amen's. He had his own table.

I went over to Amen's, went in and told the maître d' who I was and that I had an appointment with Buckalo. The maître d' took me to a table and there I saw Buckalo for the first time.

Buckalo was a short man, about five feet four inches tall, but powerfully built. He was about 55 years old at this time when I met him. He had thinning black hair. He was dressed immaculately. Beside him on the table lay a homburg, which he always wore out on the street.

Buckalo looked right at me.

"You're Larry Spellman," Buckalo said.

"That's right," I said.

"Sit down," Buckalo said.

I sat down in front of him.

"Like pasta?" Buckalo asked.

"Sure," I said. "Love it. I hear this place has great food."

"Bet your ass it does," Buckalo said. He turned to a waiter and held up two fingers, and said, "Bring a bottle of wine for my friend here."

"Thanks," I said.

"Not at all," Buckalo said,

I said, "Jimmy Roselli tells me you've done a lot for him. Advised him on the right moves."

"I've done some strategizing," Buckalo said. "Jimmy's got talent, but he's started out slow in his career. He should already be a star by now. I tell him, 'Get out there! Move! Do every show you can!' Now you see what he's doing. Some of that I set up. Booked him in nightclubs. Booked him where there were no nightclubs. *Make* the nightclubs. Like we did at Chateau Pelham. Go, go, go! Make the record! Get it on da air! Go, go, go! And now here we are. I've done all I can. I ain't in show biz. It's not my line. I'm just Jimmy's friend, trying to help. Now we need professional representation. You and me together, we can make something happen. What do you think?"

Plates of pasta and a bottle of wine arrived in the hands of waiters. In a moment our table was set.

"I think we can do something," I said. "I think Jimmy Roselli can become a star."

"As big as Sinatra?" Buckalo asked.

"Who knows?" I said. "Maybe. Sinatra's the biggest. Jimmy would have to work hard—very hard. Being the biggest isn't easy."

"No," Buckalo said, "but *aiming* to be the biggest is the only aim worth taking."

"I'm with you there," I said.

Buckalo poured the wine and we ate and drank to the success of Jimmy Roselli.

I began booking Roselli in nightclubs to season him as a performer, and to get his name out, to build some heat. I met with Buckalo twice a week for dinner at Amen's and we would strategize about Roselli's career. I began to realize how these guys got to the top. Their grammar wasn't perfect, to say the least, but they spoke to each other in clear and certain terms in a language all their own. Large amounts of money were exchanged but no legally binding documents were ever signed. I believe that's why murder was the only option. No contract means no legal recourse. Murder could close a deal in a very final way. Nothing like that ever occurred around me, nor was I ever included in decisions of that nature.

Buckalo was partners with a guy named "Fat Tony." Lucky Luciano, Vito Genovese and Frank Costello were all out of commission for one reason or another, leaving Buckalo and Fat Tony as the titular heads of the East Harlem mob, the most powerful of the Five Families of New York City. When they had problems that needed a special

Consigliere, they turned to Joe "Stretch" Straci.

It was through Buckalo that I learned how it was that the mob was able to function. The police in New York were "on the pad," a Mafia expression that indicates who in the police department was taking kickback money. These were old relationships going all the way back to Prohibition. I would venture a guess that they still exist today. When Harry Gross, one of our neighbors and the biggest bookmaker in New York, was arrested in 1969, an examination of his records revealed annual million dollar payoffs to the NYPD.

One night at dinner with Buckalo, we were joined by a Captain of the New York City Police Department. In these dinners, that Captain always kept his hat on his head at all times. I guess he wanted to be ready to go out quickly in case anything unexpected happened. Having already secured Buckalo's confidence and trust, I listened to him and the Captain speaking about how they needed to sacrifice one Mafia gambling or prostitution venue to assuage the public. Although they used certain code words, it was obvious that someone was going to get arrested and exposed.

That conversation with Buckalo and the police Captain brought about my first realization of how the network of power functions in New York City. The next morning, my brother Jerry, who was a plainclothesman for the NYC Transit Department, received a call from his superior who said that he understood that Jerry's brother was connected to some very powerful people. Jerry's superior wanted to know if he would be allowed to utilize the "connection" if the need arose. I never had to deliver on that particular request, but was able to secure my brother's favor with his boss by providing singing stars to appear at the annual fundraisers.

That same Captain gave me an honorary membership card to the Police Benevolent Society. Not long after that, I was stopped by a cop for making an illegal left turn. I flashed the card, of course, and in the conversation that followed, I revealed that my girlfriend and I were on our way to dinner in Harlem. The cop phoned ahead for us and we never got a check for our dinner that night. That's power.

Along about this time, I signed Rodney Dangerfield.

Dangerfield's real name was Cohen, but his father, who had been in vaudeville, had used the stage name Roy. So when Dangerfield started out in show business as a stand-up comedian, he went by the name Jack Roy. He plugged away in small clubs and "joints" for about ten years with little success and finally gave up show business and went into the business of selling aluminum siding door to door. He did this for a dozen or so years, all the while in a state of frustration. He wanted to get back into show business. He had a duffel bag, and every time he thought of a joke, he'd write it on a scrap of paper and throw it in the bag. After twelve years, the bag was full and he had an act-- but nobody wanted to book him. All that the bookers and agents saw was a forty year-old wanna-be, a real loser. In show business, a performer is considered old at forty, just like in sports.

I had heard of Jack Roy and how he had changed his name to Rodney Dangerfield and was trying to break into clubs late in his game. I had heard that he had gone up to the Catskills to hone his act. Dangerfield was an underdog in show business, a category of performer that was beginning to become my forte. Earlier at the office I had brought Pat Cooper to everyone's attention at a time when no one was paying any attention to him at all, but I couldn't get my bosses to share my vision. Cooper had made an album called "The Italian Wedding." My bosses refused to sign Pat Cooper and a competing agency got him and his career took off. Later, I did the same thing with Norm Crosby. I fought for Crosby, reminding everyone about how we had lost the opportunity to represent Pat Cooper. This time I was able to convince my bosses at WMA that we should represent Norm Crosby. So when I started hearing about Rodney Dangerfield, I was intrigued, and I had won enough confidence from my bosses that I now had the latitude to sign a performer on the spot if I wanted. Dangerfield was just the kind of guy I might sign on the spot if he was as good as the small buzz around him said that he was.

I went down to Greenwich Village to where I had heard Dangerfield was performing, a small place called Upstairs at the Duplex. I got there and found Dangerfield and nobody else. The place was literally empty. I introduced myself and then we waited for some customers to arrive. And we waited. And waited.

After about thirty minutes of lounging about, Dangerfield flapped his arms to his side, threw his head up, rolled his eyes, and said, "Nobody. They ain't comin'. Might as well go."

I sat still, studying Dangerfield. He was already beginning to go gray at his temples. He was dressed in a dark suit that didn't seem to fit him right. He was sweating all over his forehead.

"What do you mean 'nobody'?" I asked. "What am I? Chopped liver?"

"Gotta have more than one guy to make the jokes work," Dangerfield said.

"I'll be the judge of that," I said. "Let's see what you've got."

"My timing will be off," Dangerfield said.

"I'm here to see you," I said. "I'm not coming back a second time. This is your chance."

"Some chance," Dangerfield said.

"Just imagine an audience," I said.

"I'd need a lot more drinks to imagine an audience," Dangerfield said.

"Get up there," I said. "Show me what you've got."

"What I've got. Sheesh!" Dangerfield said. "I ain't got nothin'!"

"Get up there," I said.

"Now?" Dangerfield asked. "You mean-- *right now*?"

"Right now," I said.

Dangerfield looked up at the stage as if it was the gallows, back at me with an accusing glance, and then back up to the stage again, looking

129

at it as if he no longer recognized it, as if he didn't know what it was or why it existed. Then he stepped up into that no-man's land, grabbed the mike, and looked out across the empty room.

"Okay," Dangerfield said. "This is it. My act. And *what* an act! Would ya look at this place? A tomb has more going on it! The management advertised! They talked me up! They called their in-laws! They called their butcher! Rodney Dangerfield! Appearing Upstairs at the Duplex in person! And here I am with you, Larry Spellman, in person! Person to person! We could do an interview, man, an interview back at your place. You could ask me questions like: When's your next unemployment check due? I tell ya, this is humiliating! Not a body in sight. Hello? Can anybody hear me out there on the street? No? Nobody coming at all? Even the bums outside ain't listening to me. I tell ya, I get no respect, no respect at all. Wherever I go, whatever I do, it's the same. All my life. With my old man, I never got respect. I asked him if I could go ice skating on the lake. He told me to wait until it gets warmer. And the first time he put me on a roller coaster, he told me to stand straight up."

I was bursting apart laughing. It wasn't just what Dangerfield was saying, it was the *way* he was saying it. His whole expression rang true. It was his act, but it didn't sound like an act, it didn't look like an act, it didn't feel like an act. It felt like *Rodney Dangerfield*! Oh, boy. He kept going, kept being Dangerfield, kept climbing—- no, kept descending. He wasn't going over the top, he was hitting bottom and then digging a hole to China. He was the Total Loser, cutting himself to pieces, the sweat pouring down his face. He pulled out a handkerchief mid-sentence, ran it over his forehead and kept talking. He kept me laughing for nearly an hour!

Suddenly he was through. He just said, "If you like what I did tonight, just give me one of these." And he formed his thumb and forefinger into the "okay" sign and walked off.

I held my hand up, made the "okay" sign,

and said, "I'm signing you to the agency."

"Sh!" Dangerfield said. "Somebody will hear you and you'll ruin my reputation."

"Nobody's here," I said.

Dangerfield replied, "There's a little guy in the back who does dishes and he's got a big mouth."

I signed Rodney Dangerfield to a standard WMA contract and began booking him in nightclubs. I sent him to Detroit and all around the northeast. During this time, he kept developing his act, writing new jokes and honing the delivery of old ones.

Finally I called Dangerfield and said, "I'm booking you into the Copacabana."

"Oh," Rodney said, "that's big."

"Big as it gets," I said.

"They oughta disrespect the hell out of me there," Rodney said.

"You'll kill 'em," I said.

"That's what I mean," Rodney said. "I'm

ready. No more aluminum siding for me, buddy."

I booked Rodney at the Copa as an opening act for Sergio Franchi. When Franchi's manager heard I was putting Dangerfield in the same show as Franchi, she exploded.

"You're going to ruin Sergio Franchi's career!" she said to me.

"No, I'm not," I said. "Dangerfield will be a great opening act for Sergio Franchi. Just wait and see. I guarantee you that Dangerfield is going to kill that audience!"

Rodney Dangerfield went on to open for Sergio Franchi at the Copa and he did absolutely kill the audience. He also impressed the Copa's manager, Julie Podell. Sergio Franchi's manager calmed down.

As a result of Rodney Dangerfield's success at the Copa, Ed Sullivan took notice of him and gave Rodney a chance to audition for his TV show.

When my bosses at William Morris, Sol Shapiro and Lee Salomon, heard I was working to get Rodney Dangerfield on the *Ed Sullivan Show*, they called me in to talk.

"Dangerfield's a mess," Salomon said. "You've got to do something about the way he looks. H*e* can't go on national television in that suit he wears. It looks like he slept in it."

"What do you mean?" I asked. "That's his gimmick. That's his costume. He's the guy that don't get no respect. He's *supposed* to look that way. He's gone to great effort to look that way."

"Still," Salomon said, "he ought to look a little better. It's national television."

"Clean up Dangerfield," I said, "and you kill his comedy. You kill his act. You blunt his edge. The way he looks is an integral part of what makes his act work. Do you want to diminish that?"

Salomon and Shapiro looked at each other.

"Sounds like you feel strongly about this," Shapiro said.

"I do," I said. "My instincts say let Dangerfield keep his suit, wrinkles and all."

Salomon and Shapiro looked at each other again.

134

Then Shapiro said, "All right. He can keep his suit. Just remember: This was your idea."

"I will," I said.

Dangerfield auditioned for Sullivan in the afternoon, right after the show's dress rehearsal. He followed Dame Judith Anderson who did the death scene from Macbeth. Despite that, Dangerfield did very well during his audition. But it took somewhat over another year before he actually made his debut on *The Ed Sullivan Show*. For his first appearance he was paid $1,000.

Dangerfield killed the audience on his first Sullivan appearance. I booked him for a second appearance on the show and this time I was able to get him $1,500.

All during this period Dangerfield was still selling aluminum siding in addition to doing clubs and TV. His aluminum siding customers started recognizing him as the guy on *The Ed Sullivan Show*.

After Rodney's second appearance on *The*

Ed Sullivan Show, Sullivan came into the Copacabana where Dangerfield was working.

After Dangerfield did his act, he walked offstage and Ed Sullivan jumped up in front of him.

"You must do our show!" Sullivan declared.

"Mr. Sullivan," Rodney replied, "I'm already doing your show!"

Rodney Dangerfield did more shows for Ed Sullivan and many more shows for a lot of other people. His career, which would take him to the top, was launched.

CHAPTER SIX

The Law Finds Love

I was doing well with my many clients. Some, Like Dangerfield, looked like they were headed for real stardom.

Anna and I had parted. My breakup with her, as painful as it had been, was one of the best decisions I ever made. I and my friends Mel, Sam and Marv were each hitting our stride in our respective businesses. Money, new cars, membership in health clubs and weekend jaunts were all part of the equation. And I might add (with all humility) that each guy was better looking than the other. Custom-made suits were the norm. When we went out with our dates, we didn't just order drinks, we ordered bottles, and each of us could really hold our liquor. One weekend trip to Puerto Rico, Mel couldn't make it and a guy we knew by the name of Lenny Margolin asked if he could tag along. He told us that his friends said to him, "If you are going with those guys, you'd better catch up on your sleep."

Besides all of what was going on with what I called the "Four Horsemen of the Apocalypse," I was still going out on behalf of the office, catching shows with a nice expense account at my disposal, and I was in a position to help any girl singer get a job if I chose to do so. I could have been the Hunchback of Notre Dame and girls would still have called me to go out with me. In other words, life was good!

Along about this time I booked Jimmy Roselli into the Copacabana. The Copa was the center of the universe when it came to nightclubs, a world-famous venue that needed no sign outside its premises to proclaim its presence, only a blue awning over its door. It was on East 60th Street in New York, between Madison and Fifth Avenue.

The Copa was run by Jules Podell, a New York character right out of one of Damon Runyon's tales if there ever was one. Podell ran the best "ship" of a nightclub as anyone ever did. He was the absolute master of his domain. Podell was short, stocky and powerful. He always wore a suit. He had a ruddy face. He was like Mr. Magoo with glasses. Podell ran the Copa almost military style. Although Podell was Jewish, he was a very big contributor to the Catholic charities, and he was very close to the archdiocese of New York. But Podell spoke in a very rough and gruff manner. Everyone in show business knew Podell and knew he ruled the Copa. But everyone also knew that he was actually the front for Frank Costello who was a very big Mafia boss. Nevertheless, Podell ruled the Copa. What he said went. You never called him by his first name. It was always, "Mr. Podell." The way you best handled Julie Podell was that when you saw him walking down one side of the bar, you went to the *other* side of the bar.

Podell's employees were organized in a hierarchy. Each rank was identified by how they dressed. The top guys wore black tuxedos. The next step down of guys wore blue coats. The guys at the bottom wore red coats. Each of these coat colors represented a specific function. The black-coated tuxedo guys-- and even some of the blue-coated guys-- were tough in their own way. If there was any sort of a disturbance-- for instance: If some table was rowdy in the middle of a show, the black-coated guys would pick up the whole table and just throw everybody at that table out of the place. Even the "biggest guys" with Mafia connections never reacted when these actions of the staff would take place, because they all knew that Frank Costello was really behind it all.

The staff would snap to attention when Podell would issue an order. Podell had a place at the corner of the bar where he would sit. He wore a big ring on his pinky. Whenever he wanted something, he'd rap that ring on the bar top-- like he was ringing a bell-- and five guys would come running, saying, "Yes sir, Mr. Podell!"

When you entered the Copa, you went up a couple of steps and then you were facing the coat room. To the right was the lounge. In the lounge was a stage, and people in there could meet and have drinks before, during and after the shows.

Podell, like Buckalo, had a way of talking that could demolish the English language. God forbid anyone to make light of it! Sometimes I would kid Buckalo about the way he talked, and he never minded it, because we hit it off so well and had great rapport.

One time, one of Buckalo's associates said to me: "You know, Larry, you get away with saying things to Buckalo that, if another guy said them, he'd get killed." It's nice to have friends.

With Podell, it was an entirely different matter. When Podell slaughtered the English language, you had best not even smile. Sometimes, in listening to Podell, it was very hard to keep a straight face.

One time Podell was talking to me about booking some new entertainment at the Copa. He was seated at his usual place at the bar. His voice carried the tone of an intense, profound artistic inspiration. But what he actually said was: "Larry, I want to beef up the lounge. Go out and find me

141

some duos, three-os and four-os."

December 1966 rolled around and I had Jimmy Roselli booked into the Copa. He had made headlines in weekly *Variety* for selling out the Copa for four straight weeks. No performer, including Sinatra, ever did that. It was a triumph for Roselli.

The night I went to see Roselli perform at the Copa, it was a packed house. I was there to see him with my bosses, the brothers Nat and Harry Kalcheim. I went in and joined the Kalcheims at their table.

My bosses were there with their wives, Esther and Bea. Both of these ladies "ruled the roost" of their homes and were the definite "power behind the throne." This was also true of another top man at William Morris, Nat Lefkowitz, whose wife ruled *his* "roost." The wives dictated to these guys and the guys kowtowed to the wives. It was a hen-pecked pecking order that made you want to cackle. These men were giants in the office, but with their wives they were...*quiet*. Of the two ladies present that evening, Esther and Bea, it was Esther who was definitely the matriarch of the Kalcheims.

The two brothers, Nat and Harry, were two very different human beings. Nat Kalcheim was always immaculate in his dress and grooming. His full head of gray hair was always perfectly combed. He was of average height but had a formidable bearing, although he was very reserved and never used a four-letter word. Nat Kalcheim could also be very supportive, even fatherly. At least that was the role he took on with me. Harry Kalcheim was taller than his brother, slightly built, soft spoken. He wore glasses and looked the way college professors look in the movies.

As I sat down with the Kalcheims at their table, I noticed Ed Sullivan sitting at the table next to ours with a party of six.

Nat Kalcheim noticed me noticing Sullivan and said quietly to me, "Podell invited Sullivan. He wants him to see Roselli."

"Good," I said.

All of us had been trying to bring Roselli to the attention of Sullivan.

The evening moved forward with shop talk and family talk, all intertwined by the Kalcheims into one, homogeneous whole. While we were having dinner, Arturo Cano approached our table.

Arturo Cano was a very tall, classy-looking man with a mustache, a former diplomat from Bolivia. I already knew Cano; he was one of our WMA accounts. He had a big nightclub in Queens named The Boulevard where he played stars. Tony Bennett had played at The Boulevard, and I had booked Dionne Warwick there.

Cano came up behind me, leaned over my shoulder and rubbed my shoulders in a friendly way. He began talking to the Kalcheims and me.

I looked over my right shoulder up at him, and asked, "Arturo, where are you sitting?"

Cano nodded toward a table, and said, "I'm over there."

I looked over at Cano's table.

My head snapped back when I saw who was

sitting at the table: a knock-out beautiful redhead, a ringer for Rita Hayworth.

"Who's the redhead?" I asked.

"Would you like to meet her?" Cano asked.

I stood up.

"Excuse me," I said to the Kalcheims. "I'll be right back."

Arturo Cano brought me over to his table and said, "This is Larry Spellman, the William Morris agent I was telling you about who represents Jimmy."

Cano introduced everyone at the table. There was Cano's partner, Abe Goldstein; Cano's wife, Terry Stevens, a very tall, attractive singer who had one hit record in her career; Paul Screvane, President of the NYC Council (the second-most powerful office after the mayor); Sol Geltman who, at that time, ran the famous El San Juan Hotel in Puerto Rico, and, finally, Geltman's date-- that knock-out beautiful redhead, Rita Hayworth's double! I tried not to stare at her, but I realized, as Cano introduced her, that I couldn't take my eyes off the redhead.

Nodding toward the redhead, Cano said, "And this is Cece Straci."

Cece Straci, I thought.

"Hello," Cece said, looking straight into my eyes, looking and not looking away for one instant.

Suddenly I realized that I had sat down at the table-- probably in Arturo Cano's chair, but he said nothing. I was still looking at Cece, and she at me. Everything seemed to slow down. In the next moment, I forced myself to look away.

"See you've got Sullivan here tonight," Cano said.

"We're trying to get Jimmy on his show," I said.

"Splendid!" Cano said.

I glanced around the table again. Everyone was smiling.

"This feels like a special night," I said, "when anything could happen."

I could feel Cece watching me. I looked at her. She was looking at me, still looking and not looking away for one instant.

"Do you believe in magic?" Cano asked.

"I know it when I see it," I said, looking right at Cece. Everything came to a stop, everything but Cece and me, looking at each other and not looking away for one instant. How long we looked at each other, I'll never know. I only know that after a long time I felt Cano's hand on my shoulder again.

"Show's about to start," I said, standing up.

"Wonderful to see you again, Larry," Cano said.

"Arturo," I said, "nice to meet everyone."

My glance swept around the table at Cano's friends and stopped on Cece. She was still looking. I nodded to her, turned away, and went back to the Kalcheim's table. I wanted to speak to Cece, but I knew I couldn't make my move while everyone was sitting there.

I sat back down with the Kalcheims, and in a moment the orchestra started to play. Suddenly, Jimmy Roselli strode on to the Copa stage to thunderous applause.

From the start, his singing was superb, but throughout his entire show I kept trying to figure out how I was going to hit on Cece Straci. Every once in a while I would glance over to her table. She, like everyone else, was watching and listening to Roselli. What, I wondered, could I do to catch her attention? Then it dawned on me, just as Roselli sang his last note for the evening.

Roselli took a bow to a standing ovation.

Ed Sullivan leapt to his feet, and exclaimed, "I want him on my show next week!"

I looked over to Nat Kalcheim who was smiling at me. He gave me a nod.

Jimmy finally got offstage and the applause died down.

I said to the Kalcheims: "I want to get to Jimmy's dressing room before he gets there."

I wove rapidly through the crowd and headed backstage. There, I came upon Roselli who looked serenely exhausted.

"Great show, Jimmy!" I said.

"Thanks, Larry," Roselli said. "What's Sullivan's reaction?"

"Ecstatic!" I said. "He wants you on his show next week. You're in. Congratulations!"

"Thanks, Larry," Roselli said again.

"Thank Mr. Podell," I said. "He's the one who got Sullivan here. Listen. I've got to take care of something and then we'll hang out after your second show."

"The something is a girl," Roselli said.

"How did you know?" I asked, breaking into a smile.

"The something," Roselli said, falling into a thick Italian accent, "is-a-always a girl!"

"See you later, Jimmy!" I said with a laugh and took off toward the showroom.

Everyone in the showroom would have to get to the lounge before either going to the bar for a nightcap or exiting the front door. I positioned myself at the top of the landing of the stairway that led from the showroom to the lounge, waiting to see the redhead come up the stairs, and I timed it

149

perfectly. I saw the redhead at the foot of the stairs.

As Cece came up the stairs, I started to go down the stairs in order to pass her "accidentally on purpose."

As I passed Cece, I said, "Hello, again," shook her hand, and passed her my card, which I had in my hand all along. On the back of my card I had written, "Call me."

Cece Straci stayed for the second show.

For the second show I was now accompanied by my date, Jennifer Wells, a singer I booked now and then. She had a body that wouldn't quit and a face to match, a real knock-out blonde. Jennifer was an example of all the girls that I had been dating, enjoying a great bachelor life: custom-made suits, a mid-town apartment, always sporting a tan from the Henry Hudson Health Club of which I was a member-- and an expense account letting me wine and dine girls while covering shows for the office. In other words, I was as far away from getting laid as the nearest phone call. Marriage was the furthest thought from my mind.

But with Cece Straci, I had no idea what I was in for.

The next morning while I sat behind my desk at the office, I got a call.

"Larry Spellman," I said.

"Hello," a woman's warm voice said on the other end. It only took me a second to recognize that the voice belonged to Cece Straci.

"Cece?" I asked. "Is this Cece?"

"Yes," she said with a laugh. "How did you recognize my voice from just one word?"

"I don't know," I said. "I just did. You have a distinctive sound. I've been thinking about you all morning, hoping you'd call. I wanted to talk to you last night, but, you know, there were so many people."

"I know," Cece said. "It was a mad house. Everybody was mad about Jimmy."

"How did you like him?" I asked.

"He was great," Cece said.

"We're getting him a shot on the Sullivan

show after all," I said.

"That's wonderful," Cece said.

There was a pause on the line, and then we both spoke, almost simultaneously.

"I was wondering..." Cece started.

"I was wondering..." I started.

We both stopped.

"You first," I said.

"No," Cece said, "you first."

"Well..." I asked, "would you like to have dinner with me sometime?"

"What do you think I would like to do?" Cece asked.

"I think you would like to have dinner with me," I said.

"Why?" Cece asked.

"I don't know," I said. "Maybe because you called *me*. If you were a buyer, I'd say you wanted to buy."

"You're pretty sure of yourself," Cece said.

"I'm pretty sure of both of us," I said. "What do you say about it?"

"It?" Cece asked.

"Dinner," I said.

"I'm hungry," Cece said.

"You took the words right out of my mouth," I said. "How about I pick you up Saturday night?"

"For dinner?" Cece asked.

"Just dinner," I said. "One of my clients is appearing over at the Palm Shore Club in Brooklyn. She's Aliza Kashi, an Israeli singing star. She's got a lot of talent."

"Sounds great," Cece said. "I'd love to."

"How about I pick you up at seven?" I asked.

"I'll give you my address," Cece said.

Cece told me her address and I wrote it down. We talked a bit more, said goodbye, and hung up. I felt so light I could have floated out of the room.

Two guys were seated in my office while I took the call from Cece. They were Barry Weitz and Lloyd Kolmer. Lloyd was a look-a-like for

Lloyd Bridges. He had an unbelievable wardrobe because his father was Billy Kolmer of Kolmer-Marcus Clothiers. Both Lloyd and Barry had also been at the Copacabana the night before and they knew all about Cece Straci.

"Did I hear you right?" Barry asked. "Was that Cece Straci you were just talking to?"

"It was," I said.

"Oh, boy," Barry said.

"What do you mean 'oh, boy'?" I asked.

Barry and Lloyd laughed and shook their heads.

Lloyd asked, "Do you know who her family is?"

"No," I said. "Who's her family?"

Barry looked over at Lloyd.

"What is it with you guys?" I asked.

Lloyd said, "We know Cece."

"So?" I asked. "How do you know her?"

Lloyd said, "My father-in-law, Bart, runs the numbers racket in the northeast Bronx. He's partners with a Jewish racket guy named Sammy

Shliten. Bart's Italian, but not Mafia. Bart and Sammy pay protection money to the Mafia to insure their territorial rights."

"What's this got to do with Cece Straci?" I asked.

"Her father," Lloyd said. "He's the head of the East Harlem mob. I know her family. So does Barry, here. He's dated Cece a couple of times. I'm the one who fixed them up."

"You've dated Cece?" I asked Barry.

"We went out," Barry said. "Nothing happened. I'd advise you to be careful."

"What do you mean by that?" I asked.

"Her father," Lloyd said. "Barry's talking about her father, Joe 'Stretch' Straci. You don't want to get him mad at you. The East Harlem mob is the biggest family in the syndicate, the biggest of the five families of New York."

"Joe Straci," I said. "Yeah, I know who he is. I just didn't connect his name to Cece's."

"Well," Lloyd said, "you had better connect them."

I knew all about Joe Straci from my association with Buckalo.

"Straci's partners," Lloyd said, "were Lucky Luciano, Vito Genovese, Frank Costello and Frank Lavorse. You know, Cece's family owns Raos Italian restaurant. You've heard of Raos?"

Who, in New York, had not heard of Raos? It was legendary.

The famous Rao's is still there on 114th Street and Pleasant Avenue in East Harlem. The restaurant was started by Cece's maternal grandparents in 1898 and it is still owned to this day by Cece's brother, Ron Straci and a cousin, Frank Pellegrino. Rao's is like an old bar and grill with just some tables covered with red checkered tablecloths and some booths. The restaurant seats about 30 people. Cece's uncle, Joey Rao, was a notorious hit-man for the mob. He and "Trigger" Mike Capolla were considered the "Doberman Pinschers" of the East Harlem family.

At the time I met Cece, her uncle, Vincent

Rao was running the restaurant. He was a sensational cook. But Vincent was into other things besides his restaurant and didn't necessarily want Rao's overrun with customers all the time. But that's what he got. It parallels Mel Brooks' *Spring Time for Hitler* where they didn't want a hit show. Unbeknownst to Vincent, three nights in a row the food editor of *The New York Times* came into Rao's and gave it a rave review-- a review that any other restaurant would kill for! You had to see Vincent's reaction: "No! They can't do this to me!" Vincent didn't want a hit restaurant! Why? Because all of a sudden people like the Governor and the Police Commissioner all wanted to come there to eat! Vincent didn't want this.

On any given night at Rao's you will see the likes of Bill and Hillary Clinton, Robin Williams, Billy Crystal, and Ron Perlman of Revlon. Sitting next to such notables at other tables, you will see judges and Mafia figures like John Gotti. Woody Allen used to come into Raos often. When Woody Allen did the movie *Broadway Danny Rose*, the character played by Mia Farrow was specifically based on Vincent Rao's wife, Anne, exactly with her bouffant hair, sunglasses all the time and a cigarette holder.

It is a six month wait in order to get a reservation at Rao's. I once got a call from Ed Limato, one of the top motion picture agents in Hollywood, begging me to get him a reservation for Steve Martin. Because people are always calling Raos, begging for reservations, and because Frank Pellegrino usually has to tell them "no," Frank has acquired the nick-name "Frankie No."

On January 15th, 2011, *The New York Times* ran a front page story with the headline:

"Joey Cupcakes Is Taken Down, From the Wall"

The article, by William K. Rashbaum, tells the story of how one Joseph Urgitano, also known as "Joey Cupcakes," became the focus of an F.B.I. investigation. Urgitano had already served 19 years for manslaughter and drug dealing. During the course of the probe, the F.B.I. came into Raos with a search warrant, looking for anything having to do with "Joey Cupcakes," especially a photo of Joey that they had been told was hanging on the wall of the restaurant. They found the photo, took it down from the wall, and left with it.

Rashbaum quoted Frank Pellegrino as saying: "I have no idea what that was all about."

Rashbaum continues on his own to state: "There has been, it should be said, no suggestion that Rao's or its current owners have been implicated in any wrongdoing whatsoever."

Of course, Rao's is steeped in mob history, and that aura is part of its mystique. But the real secret to Rao's century-plus success is its food. Many swear that Rao's serves the best Italian food on the planet, and the long waiting list of people from all walks of life to get a table there supports that opinion.

That morning when I made my first date with Cece, I sat there with Lloyd and Barry, thinking about Rao's and the Straci family.

159

Lloyd said to me, "The Stracis-- you don't want any trouble from them. Did you know that Cece is divorced?"

"No," I said. "So what?"

Barry said, "You've got to be careful with a woman who's had a bad marriage. You know, her ex was there last night."

"At the very next table to Cece's," Lloyd said.

"Who is he?" I asked.

"Mike Capagnara," Lloyd said. "He's a New York State Assemblyman. Not only was he there, he was sitting there with his fiancé, the singer Connie Francis."

Barry said, "We were watching Cece to see if she would explode. We know Cece's Sicilian temper."

"You never want to get a Sicilian redhead mad at you," Lloyd said.

"Or a Sicilian redhead's father," Barry said.

"What is it with you guys?" I asked. "Are you trying to talk me out of seeing Cece? You can't do it."

"We're just telling you," Barry said, "for you own good."

"Sure," I said. "Sounds like envy to me."

"Not at all," Lloyd said. "It's just that we know your reputation around here with women. Let me caution you not to date Cece if you think you're going to play around with her the way you do with all your other bimbos."

"Yeah, Larry," Barry said, "We'd like to see you walking around healthy awhile longer."

"Ah," I said, "get out of here, ya bums. I'm busy."

They got up and went to the door, but Lloyd came back, stuck his head back in the room and said, "I'm not kidding, Larry. Remember: discretion is the better part of valor. Good luck, pal."

Then Lloyd disappeared out the door.

I sat there, looking at the telephone, thinking about Cece, about her family. Then I pushed my thoughts away and got back to work.

Roselli appeared on *The Ed Sullivan Show* and got a standing ovation, the only standing ovation in the whole history of the show. The audience response that Roselli received was even bigger than what the Beatles got when they came on the Sullivan show. People came up to me later to ask me if I had arranged plants in the audience to stand up for Roselli. They would ask me if the mob paid off the audience. These were ridiculous suggestions, claims and assertions. Anyone who knew how Sullivan distributed show tickets would have known how far-fetched the idea of a planted audience was. Sullivan ruled his show with an iron fist and would have never allowed such a thing. But more importantly, anyone who ever saw Roselli perform in person would know that he worked a very special magic on his live audiences and that he didn't need a fake audience to win a standing ovation.

A real audience was putty in Jimmy Roselli's hands.

I knew all about Jimmy Roselli. What I didn't know all about was Cece Straci. Would she be putty in my hands? I had no idea who was the putty and who was the hands, but I was about to find out.

CHAPTER SEVEN

The Ultimatum

A week later I did, in fact, keep my date with Cece Straci. You can believe I thought about her all that week.

Bill Weems of Burke and Weems was the exclusive booker for the Fairmont Hotel chain. Weems was in New York. Murray Schwartz of my office wanted Weems to see Alisha Kashi, the Israeli singing star that Murray and I had signed to William Morris.

Alisha Kashi was getting huge exposure from a multitude of appearances on *The Merv Griffin Show*. (Murray Schwartz would eventually leave William Morris to head up Merv Griffin's production company. The company would produce *Jeopardy!* and *The Wheel of Fortune*.)

I had booked Aliza Kashi at the Palm Shore Club in Brooklyn and Murray invited Weems to the dinner show in order to see Kashi. (Aliza went on to a successful career not only playing the Fairmont chain, but headlining the Copa and the Waldorf Astoria.)

At exactly seven sharp that Saturday evening of Kashi's appearance I pushed the doorbell button on Cece Straci's front door. I was standing in front of her parent's townhouse on 58th Street in Manhattan.

In a moment the door opened, and there stood Cece even more glamorous than when last I saw her. She was wearing a drop-dead gorgeous fur coat.

"Hi," Cece said.

"Wow," I couldn't help saying. The putty was already beginning to melt.

Cece and I clicked immediately. Our small talk sounded big to me. Every moment, every gesture, no matter how small, was extraordinary. This was not a date. It was an event. The two of us had something together that I can't put into words, no matter how hard I might try. This "something" had been lacking in my relationship with Anna. Cece was unlike any other woman I had ever met in my life. Not only was she knock-out beautiful, sexy and sophisticated, not only was she smart and tough-- warm and soft-- she was *on my side*. She *saw* me. She *recognized* me. She *loved* me as *I actually was*. I knew this because I felt absolutely no pressure from her for me to put on a front, to be charming and witty for the sake of being charming and witty. I was tired of being charming and witty. I wanted to just be *me*. And I could strongly sense that Cece wanted to just be *her*. She wanted both of us to just be *real*. And Cece was the realest person I had ever met in my life. Cece *was* reality.

I had always fancied myself a smooth operator with the girls until Cece made me know what I had been missing out on: *real love with a real woman*.

Yet unbeknownst to me, I might not have gone on my first date with Cece if a few other things had happened just a little differently. Let me explain.

This is what I call one of my "Hands of Fate" stories. Life has so many odd twists and turns for all of us. Who can say where we're headed, or who is helping to make our lives happen? Shakespeare said it best in Hamlet: "There is a destiny that shapes our ends, rough-hew them how we will."

Because I had been so successful in finding new talent in New York, my bosses at William Morris thought that if they sent me to California I could really strike gold. The pool of talent in Southern California was even bigger than that in New York. So in December 1966, my bosses conceived the idea of giving me my own little boutique operation for William Morris on the West Coast where I could build a stall of brand-new artists.

I was officially transferred. Everybody knew it, although I had not as yet been officially informed. David Geffen, who was the Sammy Glick of our office, knew it. He came over to congratulate me. The manager of the singing group The Lettermen was in New York at that time, and he congratulated me. In the agent business, if you've got the cramps, everybody knows about it.

The day after New Year's, I was walking down the hill from Seventh Avenue to go to the office, and the second in command at William Morris at that time, Howard Houseman, came over and congratulated me. Houseman was a brilliant lawyer that we stole away from CBS.

I said, "Mr. Houseman, Geffen-- everybody-- is congratulating me. But Mr. Kalcheim hasn't said a word to me yet."

Houseman said, "You're going! It's official. He'll probably tell you today or tomorrow."

Three days went by. Nothing.

I went to Mr. Kalchiem, and asked, "Mr. Kalcheim? Am I transferred?"

He said, "Yes, you were officially transferred. I believed in it. We all believed in it. We thought it would be a great idea. But then...I'm sitting on the couch New Year's Eve, having a drink with Nat Lefkowitz. I said, 'Nat, you know, if we transfer Spellman to California, we really don't have a strong back-up in the nightclub department. You know Spellman and Lee Salomon are our two heavies. You know something? In case something happens to Salomon, we'd better keep Spellman here.' So I cancelled it."

What's the point?

I met Cece in December 1966. If I had been transferred to California in January 1967, I never would have courted her, and our lives would have been completely different. The whole story I'm about to tell here-- the story of my life-- *would have never happened at all!* My life hinged on Nat Kalcheim's decision!

Talk about the "Hands of Fate"!

One night after one of our first few dates, I walked Cece up to the front door of her parents' townhouse. We stood there at the door, just looking at each other.

"What is it, Larry?" Cece asked.

"I was just thinking," I said. "It seems like I've always known you. But I haven't. How could that be?"

"I know what you mean," Cece said.

"You do?" I asked.

"I feel the same way about you," Cece said.

We looked into each other's eyes, and then we kissed, a long kiss, the kind they don't make anymore.

When we finally broke apart, Cece said, "Dad's been asking about you. And Mom. They want to meet you. My whole family wants to meet you."

"I want to meet them," I said.

"We have a big dinner here at the house every Sunday," Cece said.

"Then I'll come next Sunday," I said.

We kissed again, and then Cece opened the door and went inside, closing the door after her.

I went down the steps and looked back up at the house. A light was on in an upstairs window. For a moment, I imagined Joe "Stretch" Straci,

Cece's mob boss father, sitting up there in his bathrobe, maybe even smoking a cigar like Edward G. Robinson in *Little Caesar*, waiting for his daughter to come home. I immediately dismissed the image as absurd. I knew a lot of mob guys already, and they weren't like that. And anyway, Cece was a grown woman. She had even been married and divorced.

I turned and walked down the sidewalk. I walked about fifty feet and then stopped and looked back up to the Straci's townhouse.

That upstairs light was still on.

The Sunday dinner is a ritual in Italian households. Cece's parents saw that Cece was beginning to blossom and come alive again after her bitter divorce. They realized that I was making her happy. So I was invited to join them every Sunday.

Cece's brother, Ron Straci, was a tall, good-looking guy about my age. He and his first wife, Sugar Lee, were always there for Sunday dinner. Sugar was a southern girl who had been Miss New

Mexico (she was going to school there) and runner-up Miss America. Ron had met her in Clovis, New Mexico where he was stationed in the Air Force as a Captain in the Judge Advocate Corp. Sugar Lee was from Kentucky. Their marriage lasted 19 years, ending in divorce. Ron is currently married to Sharon, a very attractive lady who has displayed tremendous business acumen, successfully running Rao's Specialty Foods worldwide.

At the first of the Sunday dinners, I entered the Straci's large dining room, and Cece introduced me to her father, Joe Straci, and to her mother, Gigi. I thought Cece's parents were friendly enough, as was her brother, Ron, and his wife, Sugar. But also at the table were several other family members and friends. Some of them, I realized, were Mafia types.

Ironically, the Mafia types who came as guests to the Straci's Sunday dinners were never Italian; they were Jewish. Yes, there were a lot of Jewish racketeers who looked more like accountants, but would throw you out the window just as sure as look at you. They were men like Meyer Lansky, Bugsy Segal and Moe Daelitz who ran the Cleveland mob and the notorious Purple Gang of Detroit.

Joe Straci's major sphere of influence was the New York City garment center. You couldn't even get a truck through the garment center without Joe Straci approving it. The union officials involved with the garment center as well as the guys from the furrier's union were Joe Straci's closest allies. Because the unions could deliver votes during a campaign, the biggest political figures in New York politics would visit Joe Straci as needed. Mayor Abe Beame was seen eating a plate of pasta in the Straci's kitchen; Hugh Carey, running for governor of New York (successfully) once came to Joe Straci's showroom to speak to him. In order to explain income to the IRS, the top Mafia bosses all ran legitimate businesses. In Joe Straci's case, it was the manufacturing of ladies suits and coats. He sold to the biggest department stores in the country: Macy's, Marshall Fields in Chicago, etc. No one would refuse him. This way they avoided labor troubles!

At my first Sunday having dinner with the Stracis, I found the conversation at the table rather exploratory. Cece's parents wanted to know where I was from, who my parents were and all about my personal background.

Joe Straci was thin and tall. That is how he got his nickname, "Joe Stretch." He had thinning gray hair. He always dressed in a suit. However, at the Sunday dinner table, he would dress simply in a nice sports shirt and slacks. During the week he would always wear a shirt and tie at the dinner table, because, after dinner, he would always go up to East Harlem to discuss business with his associates, whatever that might be.

Joe Straci was cordial to me, and I was always deferential to him, calling him "Mr. Straci." (The name *Straci* is pronounced "Stray-cee," although the correct Italian pronunciation is "Strah-chee." In *The Godfather* movies I and III, they mention Joe Straci's name. Al Pacino blurts it out and calls him "Strah-chee," using the Italian pronunciation.)

Cece's mother was called by her nickname, "Gigi." Her real name was Cecilia, similar to Cece's name. Cece spelled her own name Cecelia. Even though their names were very similar, Cece was not named after her mother, but rather after a great-aunt. Gigi was an incredible cook. She could cook any kind of food: Jewish, German, Italian. The food never stopped coming out of her kitchen. And the people at her table never stopped eating what Gigi had cooked.

Things were going very well with Cece and me as the weeks flew by. Every Sunday I would be at the Straci table for Sunday dinner. I felt that the whole family liked and accepted me. So it was a shock when one day while I was at my office, a call came in. My secretary said that someone was on the line saying he was a friend, no name given. Curious, I picked up the call.

"Larry Spellman," I said.

Suddenly, the voice of Joe Straci came over the line, uttering one straightforward sentence:

"Stop seeing my daughter, or else."

And with that, Joe Straci hung up!

Naturally, I was thrown for a loop. I knew I wasn't dealing with the Boy Scouts. Now Lloyd and Barry's warnings came home to me.

I later found out what had happened with Joe Straci.

At first, Cece's father and mother liked me, and liked how I was making Cece come out of her shell after her divorce. But when they saw the two of us getting serious, Joe Straci started asking around about me, to see if I measured up as son-in-law material. What he heard about me, he didn't like.

At the time right before I met Cece, I had been associating with Joe Straci's underlings, particularly Buckalo. One of Buckalo's associates was Ben Lombardo, known behind his back as "Cock-Eyed Benny." Lombardo knew me well.

When Lombardo heard that I wanted to

marry Cece, he said to

Joe Straci: "Joe! Your daughter's gonna marry *that* guy? Are you crazy?"

Lombardo knew all about the extracurricular activities of Buckalo and me. We did a lot of the things that single men in show business do. There were women present and we were normal, healthy men, doing what normal, healthy men do with women when women are present: as in having orgies in the dressing room, having strippers perform for our dinners-- and what we called "an open door policy" in our hotel rooms, sometimes referred to as "the turnstile." (Did I say "normal and healthy"???)

Well, Cece knew all these things about me, but she loved me anyway, and she knew that I loved her, too, and that my wild days were now finished. But Joe Straci wouldn't buy that. He knew that Cece's first marriage broke up because her husband was cheating on her left and right. Joe Straci didn't want to see his daughter go through that kind of heartbreak ever again, and he was going to do everything he could to see that she didn't-- and everything Joe Straci could do was one hell of a lot.

I called Cece, and said, "I got a call from your father just now. He told me to stop seeing you, or else. Those were his exact words."

"Oh, Larry," Cece said.

"Does he say 'or else' lightly?" I asked.

"No," Cece said. "I've never heard Dad say 'or else' to anybody."

I sat silently for a moment. Cece said nothing on her end.

Then I said, "Maybe we should cool it for a while."

"Cool it?" Cece asked. "What do you mean 'cool it'?"

"Maybe," I said, "we shouldn't see each other for a while."

"Maybe not," Cece said.

"I care about you," I said.

Cece's line was silent.

"I love you," I said. "But your father--"

"Don't explain," Cece said. "I understand."

"Cece——-" I started.

"Goodbye, Larry," Cece said, and hung up.

I sat there at my desk, thinking that I had lost Cece for good. That thought was very hard to live with.

A few days later, I took a chance, and called Cece again.

I said, "I was thinking: Just because we're not seeing each other now, there's no reason we can't stay in touch by phone. No reason we can't still be friends."

"Sure, Larry," Cece said.

We talked for a while, but Cece seemed distant. Soon we hung up.

In those days, Cece worked for her father as a secretary down in the garment center. Cece would drive down there with her sister-in-law, Sugar Lee, and she would purposely go down there in a route through Manhattan that would take her by the William Morris offices, hoping to bump into me "accidentally on purpose." On occasion, she would.

179

Once in a blue moon, we would talk on the phone. They were very brief conversations. However, a lot was going on in between the lines of those brief conversations.

"Hello?"

"Hi, Larry."

"Cece!"

"How are you doing?"

"Okay. How about you?"

"Okay."

"That's good."

"Just wanted to hear your voice."

"You sound good."

"I'm not so good."

"You said you were okay."

"Okay is not so good."

"Yeah. Okay is rotten."

"Yeah. And you're okay, too?"

"Yeah, I'm okay, too."

"Bye, Larry."

"Bye, Cece."

We both knew that neither of us was ready

to quit on our relationship. I missed Cece desperately. On a couple of occasions, alone in my apartment, I caught myself crying.

During the next three months, Cece and I continued to stay in touch by phone, and at the end of the three months, September 1967, we both realized that we were truly in love and that we would continue our relationship in secret. We started meeting at a lounge in the basement of the St. Regis Hotel. We saw each other in out-of-the-way places at odd hours, places where none of our friends or family ever went. I was always careful when we went out and I don't believe we were ever followed. But although New York City and its environs is a big place, for a man like Joe Straci who knew so many people, it could be a small place. I could never tell when someone who knew Joe Straci might make an off-hand remark of the sort: "Say, Joe, I saw Cece the other night! She looked so happy. She was with that young guy-- what's his name? You know-- the guy that works at William Morris." And that would be it. I thought about the possibility of that happening, and Cece and I began eating in at my apartment more often. Fortunately, Cece was a great cook, and we had great, romantic evenings there. It was a wonderful time.

But it couldn't last.

Somehow Joe Straci found out that Cece and I were continuing to see each other. Maybe he just figured it out by seeing the change in Cece herself. When I broke up with Cece, she became depressed, stopped eating and began to lose weight. Cece's mother was worried about her. When Cece and I started dating again, Cece came alive once more. I'm sure that her father noticed the change in her. Maybe he did a little further investigating. Whatever he did, Joe Straci didn't give me another phone call. He didn't operate that way. Instead, this time, something else happened.

It was October 1967. Cece and I were just beginning one of our great romantic evenings at my apartment in Manhattan. Cece had cooked veal chops with peppers. Just as we were having our dinner, the intercom buzzed. I went over and spoke into it.

"Yes?" I asked.

The doorman's voice came over the intercom: "There's a Mr. Roselli here to see you."

I looked at Cece. She was staring at me, frozen in place.

"Roselli?" I asked, trying to figure out what to say, what to do.

"Send him up," I said.

There was nothing I could do.

You see, I realized that it was very strange in the least that Jimmy Roselli had chosen to pay me a visit at my apartment. Whenever he had visited me in the past, he had always called first. That Roselli was coming to see me at the very moment I had Cece in my apartment was too much of a coincidence. In fact, I later learned that Roselli hadn't known that Cece would be there with me, although he *was* coming to talk to me about Cece. Roselli later said that he knew Cece was in the apartment with me the moment he came down the outer hallway and smelled the aroma of the Italian food cooking.

Soon the doorbell rang and I went over and opened the door. Roselli was standing in the doorway, trying to look casual.

"Larry," Roselli said.

"Jimmy," I said. "Come on in."

Roselli came in and I closed the door. He stood, looking at Cece.

"Hi, Jimmy," Cece said.

"Good evening," Roselli said. "That smells great."

"Would you like to join us for dinner?" I asked.

"Thanks," Roselli said, "but I can't stay. I just wanted to have a little talk with you."

"Sure," I said. "Have a seat. Want to do a little strategizing on some of your bookings?"

"Uh, no," Roselli said, still standing. "It's not that. I can't stay. I've just come for a short chat. I suppose it's best you're both here now, after

184

all."

"What are you talking about?" I asked.

"This...this wasn't my idea," Roselli said slowly. "I didn't want to get involved. But I'm involved now. Boy, am I involved! I've been sent here to deliver a message."

"A message," I said. "From whom?"

"You know from whom," Roselli said. "Cece's father, Joe Straci."

Cece and I looked at each other.

"He knows, Larry," Roselli said. "He knows all about this."

Roselli waved his hand toward the kitchen and then back toward Cece.

"This?" I asked. "What do you mean by 'this'? We're just having dinner."

"That's the whole point, Larry!" Roselli said. "You and Cece are practically setting up housekeeping! If this was just a fling-- but it looks like you two are headed for the altar. You've made Joe Straci angry. Very angry."

I turned away from Roselli instinctively.

Something in me revolted at anyone telling me how to live my life. Joe Straci had pushed me. He had bent me. But he had not broken me. Joe Straci, as powerful as he was, did not know how hard it was to break me. Others had tried and failed. A power was forming in me, a power that came from Cece, from my love for her. No one, not even her father, was going to take her away from me again.

Ever.

Roselli must have sensed my absolute resolve, for he softened his tone a little.

"Larry," Roselli said, "I'm coming here as you're friend. I didn't want to come, but now that I have, I'm glad that I did, because I can see you are in need of some good advice. Advice, Larry, advice. That's all I'm offering. And, boy, do you need it! Just listen to me. You know I'm your friend. I appreciate everything you've done for me, for my career. You're a great guy! I care about both you and Cece."

Now I softened a little.

I turned back around, and said, "I know,

Jimmy."

"Larry," Roselli asked, "have you given any thought to all the problems you and Cece will be facing? You come from two entirely different worlds. You're Jewish and she's Italian and Catholic. On Sundays you're going to want lox and bagels and Cece will want pasta. The two don't mix."

I said, "We're mixing fine, Jimmy. Even you said you liked what we're cooking up."

Roselli frowned, and said, "What happens when the two of you die? You can't be buried together. You'll be in the Jewish cemetery and she'll be in the Catholic. Would that be right?"

I said, "We don't care about dying. All we care about is living."

Roselli studied my face. His own face seemed to go blank. I now think what I saw in his face was fear-- fear for what he imagined was going to happen to me.

"Larry, my friend," Roselli said, "you don't seem to understand who you're dealing with.

187

You're not dealing with me. I'm just the messenger. I've been ordered to deliver this message and it comes from Cece's father, Joe Straci, a man who never takes no for an answer. And Joe Straci says in no uncertain terms: 'Immediately stop seeing my daughter.' That's what he told me to tell you. So I'm telling you. Stop, Larry, stop. Stop right now in the name of God! Stop seeing Cece *right now*-- or you will most certainly end up in a pine box!"

Roselli and I stared into each other's eyes, but I wasn't seeing Roselli at all. I was looking directly into the eyes of Joe Straci. The eyes were cold and deadly.

Roselli looked over at Cece and then back at me. He then turned, went to the door, opened it, and went out, closing the door quietly behind him.

I looked at Cece, and she at me.

I said, "I'm going to have to talk to your father."

CHAPTER EIGHT

Show Business Marries the Mafia

The next morning after Roselli confronted me in my apartment, I decided there was only one course of action to take: I was going to marry Cece, no ifs, ands or buts. All my life people had told me that I came off like a tornado, like a bulldozer. My teacher had told me years earlier that I was a law unto myself. Was I going to let anyone intimidate me out of making the most important decision of my life-- even a Joe Straci? My answer was a clear, cold, resolute "no." Cece and I were getting married no matter what.

The question was: What was the best way of dealing with Joe Straci?

As I thought about this, I realized that Cece's father and I had never really talked, not man to man. At the Sunday dinners there had always been other people around. Usually, Cece's brother and I would do most of the talking. Joe Straci would sit, listen, and, at intervals, utter strategically sage comments. Joe Straci was a man of few words.

I knew the time had come for Joe Straci and me to have those few words.

I had the office number for the Straci showroom down at the garment center. I got a man on the line and asked to speak to Joe Straci.

"And who are you?" the man asked.

"Larry Spellman," I said.

There was a long pause.

Then the man said, "Hold the line."

I held it, held it for what seemed like many minutes. Finally, I heard some rustling on the other end, and then the voice, clear, flat and impatient—- the voice of Joe Straci.

"Yes?"

"This is Larry Spellman."

There was no sound on the line.

"Jimmy Roselli talked to me last night."

"So why are you bothering me now?"

"Mr. Straci, you know that Cece and I are

madly in love and we want to be together. Your approval matters a great deal to both Cece and I, but even without it, we are planning to marry."

Still there was no sound on the line.

I went on.

"I know you have the power to do whatever you want with me. But Cece and I are going ahead with our plans to marry no matter what you decide. We've discussed the whole thing, and we have made up our minds. We would like our marriage done the right way with your approval. We will get married no matter what. But both of us very much want your approval. We now put the matter in your hands."

The line was dead silent. The pause that followed my words seemed like an eternity to me.

Finally, to my amazement, Joe Straci said, "Well, then, you had better show up for Sunday dinner. We've got to turn mother around."

"I'll be there," I said.

"All right, then," Joe Straci said, and hung up.

I hung up my phone, and sat there wondering whether or not I had just been dreaming.

My phone conversation with Joe Straci had been no dream. At the next Sunday dinner, I found Cece's father sitting at the head of his table in what I read as a good mood. If he had been against Cece and me getting married earlier in the week, sometime over the last few days he had not only become resigned to the idea, but well-adjusted to it.

I never knew what made him change his mind, and change it so suddenly. But my guess is that he somehow realized that if Cece and I were going ahead with our plans to marry no matter what, including his not-so veiled threats, then she and I had a relationship that could stand the tests of a lifetime. I think when I stood up to Joe Straci on the phone he realized that Cece wasn't just another one of my flings. I think he had realized that I had made a lifetime commitment. And I had. Both Cece and I had committed and had drawn a line against all interlopers, including her father. As it says in the usual marriage ceremony: "What God has joined together let no man put asunder." And I think Joe Straci did believe in God and gave consideration to God's laws, despite being the Mafia boss that he was. He might've broken some of those laws, but I don't think he ever did so lightly. That's my opinion. Tough as Joe Straci was, I was to discover that he was, by personal inclination, a man of peace and something of a diplomat. Then again, maybe Joe Straci knew that anything he did to me would only adversely affect Cece. And then there was one final reason I think Joe Straci changed his mind: my sheer audacity in standing up to him. That was just the kind of thing that would have impressed Joe Straci. Looking back, I realize now that Cece and I had painted Joe Straci into a corner for the first time in his life.

Cece's mother, Gigi, came into the dining room, smiling. The moment that she recognized me at the table, her smile dropped.

"What are you doing here?" Gigi demanded of me.

"I invited him," Joe Straci said. "He's having dinner with us."

"Why?" Gigi asked.

"Larry has asked me for Cece's hand in marriage," Joe Straci said, "and I've given my consent."

"Oh, no!" Gigi cried, collapsing into the chair beside her husband. "Oh, no! How could you? How could you decide without talking to me first? Her own mother!"

"Mom—- " Cece started to say.

Gigi cut her off.

"*I'm* talking here," Gigi said, holding up her hand. "What happened to Larry-that-no-good-so-and-so? That Larry who wasn't good enough to breathe the same air as our daughter?"

Joe Straci shrugged.

"What's become of you, Joe?" Gigi asked in despair.

"I thought it over," Joe Straci said, "and

made my decision. This is America. It's the twentieth century. Today young people decide for themselves who they're going to marry. Parents have to accept their decisions. Anyway, Larry and I have talked things over and I'm satisfied he's the right man for Cece. That's all there is to it."

"That's all there is to it?" Gigi asked incredulously.

"That's all there is to it as far as I'm concerned," Joe Straci said.

"What about me?" Gigi asked heatedly. "Don't I have a say?"

"Of course you have a say," Joe Straci replied. "That's why we're here, so you can say. So say."

"I say *no!*" Gigi declared. "That's a-what I say! No. No. No!"

Gigi looked over at Cece and then at me.

"There he is!" Gigi said, pointing her finger right at me. "What happened to Larry That No-Good So-and-So?"

"I'm right here," I said. "I'm not perfect."

"Not perfect?" Gigi asked with a bitter laugh. "I'll say! You're a no-good so-and-so. I'm a lady and I don't say the bad words, not at my own table, but you know what I mean! I need the bad words right now to talk to a so-and-so! Just look at you-- you-- you-- !"

"Mom-- " Cece started to say.

Gigi cut her off.

"*I'm* talking here," Gigi said, holding up her hand.

"I love your daughter, Mrs. Straci," I said. "Cece and I are in love with each other. We're right for each other. I know what you think about me. But all I care about is Cece now. She's the only woman in my life. She's going to be the only woman in my life for as long as we're alive. I'm going to do everything in my power to make Cece happy, to give her a good life. I want for her what you want for her. And both of us want to be married in the proper way, with your blessing."

Gigi sat, fuming at me, shaking her head.

"If I am so terrible," I asked, "why do you

think Cece wants to marry me? What do you think she sees in me?"

"She *don't* see sometimes!" Gigi declaimed.

"I love Larry, Mom," Cece said quietly, but with an incredible strength and resolve that stopped her mother cold.
"Don't you remember how I was when I stopped seeing him? Mom. Don't you remember?"

Gigi's face softened. I saw her eyes light up. I saw how much she loved her daughter.

"I remember," Gigi said.

Cece and Gigi sat looking at each other. Suddenly they both reached out at the same instant and clasped each other's hand.

"Do you want to see me that way again?" Cece asked her mother.

"No," Gigi whispered. "I don't ever want to see you that way again."

"Then say 'yes,' Mom," Cece said.

Cece reached over to me with her other hand, took my hand in her own, and then brought my hand over to touch her other hand clasped in the hand of her mother. We held our hands across the table.

"Say 'yes,' Mom," Cece said again. "Say 'yes' to love-- and life."

Gigi looked at Cece and me, her eyes starting to fill with tears.

"Love...and life," Gigi said.

"Love and life," Cece said.

"Love and life," I said.

"Say 'yes,' Mom," Cece said. "Say 'yes.'"

Tears rolled down Gigi's cheeks. Her lips trembled. Then she slowly opened her mouth.

"Yes," Gigi said, slowly, solemnly. "Yes. Yes. Yes! Life is not perfect. Love is not perfect. And my future son-in-law, he's a not-so-perfect. You take care of my Cece, you not-so-perfect so-and-so!"

"I will, Mrs. Straci," I said.

"No more 'Mrs. Straci,'" Gigi said. "From now on, you will call me 'Mom.' You going to be my son-in-law."

"Mom," I said.

Gigi nodded, smiling through her tears. Cece laughed.

Joe Straci said, "Let's eat."

Gigi got up and went to the kitchen, and Cece went after her. Several more guests showed up, and we all sat down to a big feast. All tension in the air had dissipated, replaced by the clarity of family harmony, true happiness.

I later learned that Josie, one of Gigi's friends at her country club, had also been lobbying for Cece and me.

Josie had said, "Gigi, forget the Jewish-Catholic thing. We all go to heaven to meet God. We just go on different trains."

In perfect Italian tradition, Gigi immediately began making elaborate wedding plans. Again, I saw that I was going to have to take a bold position.

"I know the perfect place for the reception!" Gigi exclaimed. "I'll call them tomorrow!"

"Hold on there a minute, Mom," I said.

"What do you mean 'hold on'?" Gigi asked.

"This wedding is going to be my party," I

said. "I'm going to plan it, book it and pay for it. This wedding is my baby. I've played at a million weddings as a musician, and I've decided long ago that when I got married, it would never be like all the other weddings where I've played. I want our wedding to be different and memorable."

"But-- " Gigi started to say.

Joe Straci cut her off.

"*Larry's* talking here," Joe Straci said, holding up his hand.

Gigi's head snapped over to look at Joe.

Everyone at the table burst out laughing. Gigi looked around in confusion and then suddenly started laughing too.

Now that I had Cece's parent's blessing on our wedding, I informed my side of the family that I was getting married. My mother and father had already passed away. My mother had passed away in 1960. If my parents had been alive, there would have truly been a problem. My parents were Old World Orthodox Jews. In their view of the world, one never married outside the faith. If a son or daughter did so, he or she was considered as dead. The parents would even say the Mourner's Prayer. Although I wasn't so orthodox in this way, I treasured my Jewish heritage and religion and held them close to me. I wanted my brothers and sisters to accept my marriage to Cece, and they did immediately. That is, all with the exception of my brother, Robby. However even he gradually came around to accepting my marriage.

Several months later, I was at a business meeting with Murray Shapiro when he took a call while I was sitting in his office. The call came from the man who had been Cece's date the night we met, Sol Geltman.

I said to Murray: "Hey! I know him. Let me say a word."

Murray gave me the phone.

"Hey, Sol," I said. "This is Larry Spellman. Remember me? The Copa, December 1966?"

"Hey, sure," Sol said. "How are you

doing?"

"I'm doing great," I said. "What are you doing now?"

"Well," Sol said, "I've become the senior vice-president of the Holland-America Cruise Line."

"No kidding," I said. "That's great."

"What are you doing now?" Sol asked.

"Ha!" I said. "Would you believe I've got something really big going?"

"You've signed a big star?" Sol asked.

"Much, much bigger than that," I said. "Remember your date that was with you at the Copa?"

"Cece Straci?" Sol asked. "Do you think I could forget her? Of course I remember Cece! I ought to call her!"

"Too late," I said. "I'm going to marry her!"

"Wow!" Sol said. "I am impressed. You stole her from me! What an operator!"

"I had to, Sol," I said. "It was destiny."

"It had to be," Sol said. "The only explanation. Otherwise, how could she pass me up?"

"Say, Sol," I said. "A light bulb just went off in my head! I've been racking my brains, trying to plan our wedding and all of a sudden the solution has come to me just now as we're talking! You know what? *You* are the solution!"

"I am?" Sol asked. "I've never been a solution before. This is new."

"Your cruise lines," I said. "Your ships. I want to have our wedding on board one of your ships!"

"That's a great idea!" Sol said. "Half of a great idea. I'll supply the other half. Let me handle the whole thing, Larry. I know exactly what you want."

"This is it!" I said. "This is what I've been looking for! Imagine if you hadn't called just now."

"It's more of that destiny of yours," Sol said.

"That's what it has to be," I said.

Sol Geltman arranged our whole wedding

aboard the *U.S.S. Constitution*, as well as the Caribbean cruise Cece and I took when our wedding guests disembarked. Not only that, but Sol picked up the tab for everything! What a guy! He loses the girl and makes a life-long friend of her new husband!

On the morning of my wedding I dressed in my blue suit. I had my suitcase already packed, ready to go. Jimmy Roselli and one of my fellow William Morris agents, Dennis Paget, picked me up at my apartment and drove me to the pier where the *U.S.S. Constitution* was docked. It was over on the shore of the Hudson River near 46th Street.

Cece and all her entourage were already on the ship in their staterooms getting dressed.

When we got to the pier, Roselli, Paget and I got out of the car, and Paget and I went up the gangplank, I carrying my suitcase. Roselli stayed on the pier. He had stopped to speak to his piano player who he had invited. Roselli was going to sing. He and his pianist were discussing the program of songs. Somebody on the ship's staff took my suitcase to the wedding suite, and then we all went right in to the reception.

In Jewish weddings the party starts before the wedding ceremony. You have hors d'oeuvres, the bar is open, there's music, and you warm everybody up for forty-five minutes to an hour. Then you go in to another room where the seats are laid out and an altar is set up for the ceremony. After the ceremony you come back into the other room for a dinner buffet.

The reception began at noon, and we all went in for the wedding ceremony at 12:45 pm. Roselli was my best man, Cece's sister-in-law, Sugar Lee, was the matron of honor. There were about 60 or 70 guests in attendance. The guests consisted of Cece's family, my family (including my brother Robby who finally decided to attend) and many friends and business associates.

Our wedding party was peppered with notables like Rodney Dangerfield, Marilyn May, Bobby Vinton, writer Jimmy Breslin and, of course,

Jimmy Roselli. On Cece's side of the family some of the most notorious mob bosses also attended. The Italian tradition of giving envelopes of money was in full force that afternoon. My bosses from William Morris were impressed when they saw that a very important businessman and philanthropist had come to my wedding. He was E.M. Loewe who owned the Latin Quarter. Loewe was one of the WMA accounts.

My bosses were knocked out when they saw who was going to perform the wedding ceremony. It was Nat Sobel, one of the most powerful judges in New York, and a regular guest at the Straci Sunday dinners. Sobel was then in his sixties, a stocky man, and, in his youth, an amateur boxer. Nat Sobel was a surrogate judge of Kings County. They were the ones who probated everything and dispensed all the estates where there were no wills. So these surrogate judges like Nat Sobel were very powerful. Nat Sobel also had written books and was a power in the Democratic Party. When my bosses saw Nat Sobel standing up there officiating my wedding, they were very impressed.

The ceremony began with Joe Straci walking Cece up the aisle. I walked down to meet them, to take her from him.

As I took Cece's arm, I said, "I'll take care of her now."

Joe Straci replied, "You'd better."

The wedding ceremony went off without a hitch. It was beautiful.

In what seemed an amazingly short time, Nat Sobel said, "I now pronounce you man and wife. You may kiss the bride."

Cece was absolutely radiant. I kissed her, and then we turned.

Joe Straci was looking right at us. Cece's mother, Gigi, had tears on her face.

Cece and I went straight to the reception area. I danced with Cece and then she danced with her father. The whole afternoon we all ate, danced and drank.

About 3 pm, Jimmy Roselli got up to sing. First, he started off with *Sorento*, a classic song in the repertoire of Italian music. He killed the people with it. Then he segued into *My Yiddisha Mama*. Well, I started crying like a baby. I thought of my mother who had passed away in 1960. After the song, everybody was silent, dead silent. Everybody was staring at me. I didn't realize it at the time, because I was sitting right there, facing Jimmy Roselli.

In the silence, I suddenly got up and went over to the bandleader, and said, "Cy, come on, let's get this thing going!
Get the music going!"

Cy started the band off with a lively tune.

I passed the bartender, and said, "Give me a stiff drink."

I later found out my mother-in-law, Gigi, went over to my sister who was the oldest in my family, and said, "Don't worry, Essie. I'll feed him. I'll take care of him."

A month later, Joe Straci said to me regarding this moment: "I had to turn away. I couldn't look."

I really cried there like a baby for my mother. Cece came over and put her arms around me. We held each other, and the music lifted us up, up high, to a place of our own.

It was a great party, the wedding I had always wanted.

Around 5 o'clock, everybody in the wedding party disembarked. Cece threw the bouquet over the railing of the ship and down to the dock where my niece caught it.

Cece and I waved to the crowd at dockside as our ship pulled away, plying the waters of the Hudson River. We were on our way to the Caribbean. We were bound for Puerto Rico, St. Thomas and St. Martin. We watched the people at dockside shrink away. Then the buildings of New York stood back from us. Then the Statue of Liberty waved goodbye to us with her torch.

Then we were off on the voyage of the rest of our lives.

The cruise was wonderful. In those days, on board ship you got dressed. Two nights were black tie, very classy, very elegant. The food and the service were the very best.

Everything was going great on the cruise until just before we got home. Two days before we disembarked, Cece got very sick.

She sat up in bed, gasping for breath. I was terrified for her and immediately called the ship's doctor. The doctor examined her, but he couldn't figure out what was wrong.

We contacted a doctor in New Jersey who was a friend of the family.

He said: "Bundle her up and get her to the hospital in Teaneck."

I rushed her there immediately.

CHAPTER NINE

Central Park South

Cece's parents came to the hospital in Teaneck, New Jersey, and we conferred with the doctor. He had no idea what was causing Cece's shortness of breath, but he said they were in the process of giving her a battery of tests.

"You don't even have a clue?" I asked.

"I'm afraid not," the doctor said. "Medical science moves slowly. We can't guess on something like this. We have to know. The only way we can know is to do tests. I'd advise all of you to get some rest yourselves. She's on oxygen now and stable. We'll keep you informed."

The doctor walked away, leaving me with Cece's parents standing in the hall. Both of them looked drained.

"The doctor's right," Joe Straci said. "There's nothing we can do here. Let's go."

We all walked down the long hallway

together and out of the hospital. I really was their son-in-law now, and I really was a married man with a wife in the hospital. I felt all of it like a heavy weight.

Cece was hospitalized for many days. Over this period of time her condition gradually improved. Finally, the doctor called me in, and I brought Cece's parents with me. We sat down in his office.

He said, "We've finally figured out what's wrong with your wife. It's a rather rare condition called Burkside Syndrome."

I looked over to Cece's parents. They were staring at the doctor blankly. I looked back to the doctor.

"Just what does that mean?" I asked. "Is it serious?"

"Well," the doctor said, "it can be, given the right conditions, but not in your wife's case. It's basically a reaction to toxins introduced into the lungs."

"Toxins?" Joe Straci asked. "You mean

poison?"

"Yes," the doctor said. "Cece has been poisoned, you might say."

"By who?" Joe Straci demanded. "How? Where?"

"By herself," the doctor said.

"What?" I asked.

"Cece poisoned herself accidentally, we believe," the doctor said.

"How could she poison herself accidentally?" Joe Straci demanded to know.

"By using too much hairspray," the doctor said.

"Hairspray?" I asked.

"I talked to her," the doctor said. "It seems she was using a lot of hairspray in your stateroom on board the ship."

"Well, sure," I said. "Women use lots of hairspray all the time, but how could it poison Cece?"

"The combination of the close quarters," the doctor said, "the amount of hairspray and your wife's susceptibility to the syndrome induced the reaction in the lungs."

"You're saying Cece is allergic to hairspray?" I asked.

"You might say that," the doctor said. "She should be careful using it from now on."

"Is she going to be all right?" I asked. "Is she going to recover completely?"

"I think so," the doctor said, "but we want to keep her here a little longer."

We were all relieved to hear the news. I was confident that Cece would be all right. But it was a different story with Cece's mother, Gigi. Years earlier, Cece had a first cousin who had died at the age of 29, the same age Cece was when she married me and got sick. The first cousin was a brilliant physicist working for the government, and before she died of her illness, she had one of her legs amputated. Cece's mother, Gigi, had that Italian superstition. Because Cece was now the same age as the first cousin was when she died, Gigi feared that Cece might share the cousin's fate. There was a statue of the Virgin Mary there at the hospital in Teaneck, and so every time Gigi came to the hospital, she would bow before it, hoping to save her daughter's life through an intercession of the Virgin Mary.

At the end of ten days Cece showed no further symptoms, and so the doctors released her from the hospital. Finally we were able to come home to our new apartment on Central Park South.

Just before I got married, I had spoken to my bosses about the idea of William Morris establishing a personal appearance department in London. The whole point of my idea was that I assumed I would be the agent that they would send to London to make it happen. My bosses liked my idea of the London-based department, but instead of sending me, the London job was delegated to another agent in the office, Larry Curzon. He left for London at the same time that I got married. So when Cece got out of the hospital, we took over Larry Curzon's apartment. It was on the fourth floor of an elegant building in a prime location: at the corner of Seventh Avenue and 59th Street-- Central Park South. It had a doorman. You walked out the front door of the apartment and you were facing Central Park. It was New York at its best. We lived there happily for the next four years.

It was during these years that I really got to see firsthand how things worked and how things happened in New York City. There was a complex and subtle interweaving between different sectors of society: the mob, local and state government, unions, businesses-- and particularly the show business of nightclubs. People on the outside of this complex tapestry would see separations and sharp dividing lines. But if you were inside any of these worlds, you saw that everything connected to everything else; everything that happened in one sector tended to affect everything else in the tapestry.

The mob made a ton of money in Prohibition days. They were into trucking in order to transport the liquor. They had their own truck drivers. So, as an off-shoot, they were in the trucking business. When Prohibition ended, it was a natural sequence for them to take advantage of their knowledge and expertise in the trucking industry, and that was how they helped organize the Teamsters. This was one way they could control what was going on, because if you didn't adhere to what the union truckers wanted, you didn't get delivery of your goods. An integral part of the infrastructure of the United States—- trucking-- largely grew out of what the mob had been doing in the Prohibition Era. Before then, there were no paved roads, no motorized shipping vehicles. There were only railroads going to major cities. But then in the 1920s the paved road system was built, and the trucking industry began with the transport of Prohibition liquor. By controlling the trucks, the biggest companies who would soon want their products shipped in this new way would have to kowtow to whoever controlled the trucks. The Mafia guys, by virtue of controlling the unions, controlled a lot of the economy that moved America. The mob had all this money. So they started to invest in legitimate businesses-- nightclubs, theaters. They invested in big hotel-casinos in Cuba.

The biggest manifestation of their investments was Las Vegas. That was when Bugsy Segal realized what Vegas could be.

Here is a classic example of how even the biggest guys like Napoleon or Caesar can lose their heads over a "broad." What caused Bugsy Segal's demise was the wild girl Virginia Hill.

The original capitalization of the Flamingo Hotel in Las Vegas was with Mafia money. It was Bugsy Segal's dream and the mafia's dough. The dream looked like it was going to succeed, but Bugsy's girlfriend, Virginia Hill, started ruining everything. By the time Segal got through all Virginia Hill's craziness and giving her everything she wanted, the mob found out that she was stealing money from Bugsy. The total sum ran up to four million. With Virginia Hill calling the shots, Bugsy was out of control. He lost his mind over this "broad." No matter what his friends Meyer Lansky and Joe Adonis said to him, he went right ahead serving the whims of Virginia Hill. Bugsy lost his cool and lost his perspective and his friends finally "eliminated" him.

My father-in-law and mother-in-law knew Bugsy Segal very well. My mother-in-law used to come out to California with Cece when my wife was a kid. They would come to visit my mother-in-law's sister, Rose and her husband, Artie Sarno. He was a big boss up in New England. He and his wife ran all over the world to get away from other mobs (a story I'll tell shortly). Artie and Rose settled in Los Angeles. My mother-in-law would go out to LA with Cece on the train because she wouldn't fly. Whenever my mother-in-law would come out to California, she would always have lunch with Bugsy Segal at Romanoffs. My mother-in-law always said that Bugsy Segal was the handsomest guy you would ever want to meet.

Bugsy came from the East Side of New

York. They had a triumvirate: Meyer Lansky, Ben Segal (you wouldn't say "Bugsy" to his face) and Lucky Luciano. They grew up together around Orchard Street, Delancey Street. It was a place of tenements and Old World immigrants, almost ghetto-like. They all were poor, and, as kids, they turned to crime.

Now back to Cece's Aunt Rose and Uncle Artie: Artie and Rose had run all the way around the globe to escape the wrath of the mob. They had fled to Paris and then to Australia before it was finally safe enough for them to return to the US. When they came back to the States, they settled in LA. When Cece and I moved to LA, we became very close to Cece's Aunt Rose and Uncle Artie.

Remember that Cece's mother, Gigi, was the sister of the notorious mob hit-man Joey Rao. Gigi and her sister Rose had yet another sister, Netty, as well as two other brothers, Vincent and Louie. But of all of the Raos, it was Joey who was the most feared. He was called the mob's "Doberman Pincher."

221

In his heyday, Rose's husband, Artie Sarno, had been partners with Sam Cafaro. They were big mafia bosses covering the western half of Massachusetts. I coincidentally met Cafaro when I was in West Springfield, Massachusetts with Al Martino who was headlining a theatre there. Cafaro invited us to lunch and that's when I told him that I was Sarno's nephew and who I was married to.

Cafaro and Sarno's function was transporting the booze during prohibition for the different ports of entry, wherever they could buy "muscle" or influence. Even the Gulf of Mexico was in their sphere of influence. Why? Because Louisiana was the most corrupt state in the Union, and money talked. It went all the way to the top. Let's put it this way: when Artie married Rose at the Waldorf Astoria, Governor Huey Long of Louisiana sent them a $10,000 wedding gift!

I never got the story straight, but Artie did something tantamount to a double-cross with members of his mob, and that's why he and Rose had to run.

The story my mother-in-law, Gigi, told me is that the "boys" caught up with Artie and Rose as they were boarding the ship in New York for France. What saved Artie was that Rose shielded Artie with her body as guns were drawn. She said, "You'll have to kill me first." Being that Rose's brother was the notorious Joey Rao, the "boys" backed off!

One night after we had settled in at our apartment on Central Park South, Cece and I went to see Jimmy Roselli for his opening at Arturo Cano's The Boulevard nightclub in Queens. We were joined by Cece's parents, as well as Cece's brother, Ron, and his wife, Sugar. As soon as we got seated at our table, in walked Jimmy Doyle (another nickname...for some reason a lot of Mafia figures adopted Irish nicknames).

Doyle had just come out of prison and hadn't seen my father-in-law in ages, so they really embraced. My father-in-law introduced me as his new son-in-law who just happened to be Jimmy

Roselli's agent.   After all, Doyle came there because it was Jimmy Roselli's opening.

Two weeks after I met Doyle at The Boulevard, I stopped in to the Copa for a meeting with Julie Podell. I saw Doyle at the bar in the lounge, talking to a very stately gentleman. I didn't want to interrupt, but Doyle saw me, and, since I had just met him only two weeks earlier, I thought I should go over and say hello. So I did.

"Hey," Doyle said, "it's Larry, right? Larry Spellman?"

"That's right," I said.

Doyle turned to the man to whom he had been talking, and said to him, "This is Joe's new son-in-law."

"Really," the stately gentleman said, obviously impressed.

Doyle didn't say, "Joe Straci." He just said, "Joe," with the presumption that the man would know exactly who he was talking about. And the man *did*. The man knew *exactly* who "Joe" was.

Can you imagine who this stately gentleman

was?

He was Joe Walsh, *the former Police Commissioner of New York City*!

While we were talking, Johnny Dio, who ran the garment center for the mob, (they made a movie of his life) came over and said to me, "Hey kid, I love your tie."

Knowing who he was, I was somewhat intimidated and immediately offered to give it to him. He jokingly refused and proceeded to join the gathering.

Apparently, when Dio saw me talking to Doyle and Walsh, he asked one of his cronies who I was, and being one of my father-in-law's good friends he decided to tease me a little bit.

Never, ever over-staying your welcome in this type of situation, I gracefully excused myself so that they could continue to talk about the things they were there to talk about.

Since my father-in-law "ran" the garment center in New York, all the Straci's social circle were Jews. (Joe Straci was well entrenched in all of the unions, including the Furriers union, even though the Furriers weren't considered a part of the garment center.)

Every summer when Cece and her brother Ron were young, the Stracis would accompany their Jewish friends for three weeks to the famous Concord Hotel in the Catskills. The owner of the hotel was "old man Warnerick," as he was referred to. The Warnerick family also owned a well-known men's hair tonic, JERIS. Talk about creative maneuvers! I found out through my own sources that my father-in-law never got a bill from the hotel for their entire stay. I once asked my father-in-law if that story was correct, and...how come? He said to me: "You don't think there was hair tonic in those bottles, do you?"

Because of my marriage to Cece, a lot of Mafia guys interested in show business would call me to see if I could help them with some performer they were promoting.

Along about this time, two Mafia guys named "Buddy" and "Tony" called me. They were backing a singer named Vic Venturo. I told them that I might be able to help them, so they came over to the office to talk to me further about Venturo. I ended up going to see Venturo perform. I thought he was a good enough singer that I could book him in local joints.

Buddy was very appreciative of me setting up these dates for them. I loved my Plymouth convertible, but Buddy had a car leasing business, and he said to me: "Sell your car. Pick up whatever you can for it. I'm going to give you a Caddy convertible to drive around free of charge." I took him up on his offer.

The car was nice, but there was only so much I could do for Vic with his limited talents and performing skills. I did what I could for him, and that was the end of it.

But then....

A couple of years later, I was in the Persian Room, the showroom of the Plaza Hotel, and I saw

Tony in the corner with some lady.

I went over, and said, "Hey Tony! How are you? How's Buddy?"

"Oh," Tony said, "Buddy passed away."

"Oh really," I said. "That's too bad. So what's going on with you?"

And-- only in America!

This was one of those guys who spoke in "dese, dem, and dose."

Tony said, "I'm in the cuhcus business."

I asked, "The *what*?"

Tony said, "Cuhcus."

I didn't know what he was saying.

Now remember, I'm very Jewish, and I'm very religious, and on holidays I used to go to temple, and I knew what a *Succoth* was. It was a special hut that they would build outside a synagogue to celebrate the festival of the harvest. But I had no idea what a "cuhcus" was.

So I said, "What are you talking about?"

Tony replied, "You know, Larry, this thing with the Jews? They got this festival and build the

228

huts? I got the contract with all the temples! All the temples in the whole city!"

I couldn't believe my ears! I thought: the Mafia guys are even getting into *that*!

The Mafia had gotten into the "*Succoth* business"!

Where does it stop?

The Mafia influence was in all sorts of legitimate businesses. They got involved with unions, garbage collection, longshoremen, even the *Succoth* business! They started to run catering halls that held Jewish weddings and bar mitzvahs, and they would naturally put in as waiters and maître d's their own kind of "guys."

I'll never forget this: It happened in my early years at William Morris, when I was still working weekends as a musician. I was playing a catering hall in Hillside, Queens called the Hillside Caterers. The maître d' was a little Italian guy who looked like Joe Pesci; he even sounded like him.

Part of the ritual at any one of these affairs

whether it was a wedding or bar mitzvah was that the first thing before anybody eats, they usually called up the grandfather or some elder person to make the *mutzih* of the *challah*, the blessing of the bread.

In this particular affair, I, acting as the bandleader, was supposed to make the announcement: "Please be seated, be quiet. Grandpa so-and-so is going to make the *mutzih* of the *challah*."

I couldn't get this crowd quiet for nothing. They were the most rowdy——-

The little "Joe Pesci," the little maître d' comes up to me, grabs the microphone, and bellows into it with a thick Italian accent like a big Mafia guy out on the street corner: "AY! WUH CHA' S'LET D'EM MAKE DA' MERTSY ON DA' CAHLAH?!!!"

I thought I'd fall over, laughing.

I thought: Only in America!

Everyone at William Morris knew I was

representing Jimmy Roselli, Al Martino and Enzo Stuarti. All the Italian singers were coming to me. Everybody at the office knew I had contact with the Mafia guys. They all knew me in the office as "the guy to go to," if you wanted to get something done.

I went to Philadelphia to a club, a real Mafia "joint" called The Zu Zu Club. It was on Walnut Street, run by two Mafia guys, Sam LaRose and Gene Cella.

We had a problem. The singer Julius LaRosa wanted to leave the club and not fulfill his engagement. Why? Well, The Zu Zu Club was one of those places where you not only stepped down physically to enter it, but you stepped down socially, as well. Let's say it had a number of rough edges, and they all protruded. So LaRosa hated the place and wanted to quit.

And he did quit.

The owners of the club were looking for retribution. Somebody had to pay and pay in a Big Way. Maybe it would be LaRosa. Maybe it would be me.

Fortunately, the owners asked somebody in Philadelphia: "Who's this Larry Spellman?"

And they were told by those who knew: "It would be a good idea if you guys got friendlier with him, because of his father-in-law."

So the owners of The Zu Zu Club, Sam LaRose and Gene Cella, actually showed up at my home at Central Park South.

The doorman rang, and said, "There are two gentlemen here from Philadelphia to see you."

I knew who they were, and wasn't really surprised that they had showed up. I went down to see them. We had a nice chat, smoothed things over, and we got very friendly.

Three or four months later, Howie Weiss, a TV agent for the William Morris office, had to go to that same club in Philadelphia to see some act. He came back and told everybody what had happened to him down at The Zu Zu Club. His tale spread throughout the whole office like wildfire. Here is his tale:

Howie Weiss stepped down into The Zu Zu

Club, sat on a barstool, and ordered a drink. As he was nursing his cocktail, he started looking around the place. All he could see were a few disreputable characters and one well-dressed guy who seemed to own the place. The well-dressed guy kept staring at Howie. Howie would look away, sip his drink, and then look back at the well-dressed guy who would still be staring at him. This well-dressed guy turned out to be Gene Cella. These Mafia guys were always suspicious of any new face that would enter their establishments, and Cella did not recognize Howie. So Cella had his eye on him.

Finally, Cella came over to Howie, and said, "I own this club. Who are you?"

Howie replied, "I'm Howie Weiss with the William Morris Agency."

Cella's whole demeanor changed, and he said, "William Morris? Then you must work with Larry Spellman."

Weiss said, "That's right."

Cella said to the bartender: "This guy is our guest. No check. And make sure his glass is always full."

This story passed all over the William Morris office, and everybody was saying, "Man, Spellman is really hot with the Mafia!"

Well, my father-in-law was the one hot with the Mafia, and a little of it rubbed off on me, because of my connection to him. Show business is a conspicuous business, and so every little thing like this can be blown out of proportion. It's not like I planned these things. I didn't manufacture them, but if they were going to exist, I was going to capitalize on them. So I let everybody at the office think what they wanted to think. I didn't explain. I didn't qualify. I just walked around like... *I am The Guy*! I think maybe a few suspected I *was The Guy*!

But a lot of the mob guys would like to make a show of exhibiting their power, to prove that they were like the Godfather in the movies.

An example of this was an incident that happened to me on Long Island. I was at one of the clubs I was booking at that time, the San Su San. I had booked Al Martino there as the headliner. In the audience was a mob boss, not a big boss, but more like a lieutenant. His name was Andy Russo.

Somehow I had found out that Russo knew the movie producer Ralph Serpio who had co-produced the smash-hit movie *Halloween*. I was trying to get to Ralph Serpio to pitch him something.

After the show, about one or two o'clock in the morning, I got into a conversation with Russo, and in the course of our conversation I casually mentioned that I was interested in trying to contact Serpio.

Russo suddenly said to me: "You want Ralph Serpio? Right now? Right now? You want him here now? I'll get him here right now! I can do it!"

I said, "Come on, it's two o'clock in the morning! I don't want to bother him."

Russo said, "He's coming here right now."

Russo immediately called Serpio on the

phone.

Russo said, "Hey! Get over here! Now. I'm at the San Su San Club!"

Then Russo hung up.

"Now," Russo said, "watch. He'll be here. Take him about twenty minutes."

"Twenty minutes!" I said.

"If he drives fast," Russo said. "And he'll drive fast."

Sure enough, just about exactly twenty minutes later in came Ralph Serpio. He came in wearing his overcoat on top of his pajamas.

Serpio spoke to Russo and then came and set down next to me.

I said, "Ralph, I didn't mean to get you up out of bed."

He said, "No, I understand."

We talked, but I wasn't able to get anything going with him, and I wasn't surprised. Two-thirty in the morning is a bad time to make a pitch.

Obviously, Ralph Serpio was beholding to Andy Russo. Serpio must have made those movies with Mafia money, and Andy Russo wanted his money's worth.

During the months right after I married Cece, my world at William Morris was blossoming. I was working very hard, and my clients were doing very well. Because of the success I had had in proving the value of clients that the office didn't want, I had become established as the guy who could get a new, unknown performer's career rolling.

Besides Rodney Dangerfield, I had Marilyn May.

Marilyn May's manager brought her around to Danny Segal's nightclub The Living Room, a place that showcased a lot of future stars. I flipped when I heard her for the first time there. She had a vocal presence like a great jazz musician. She gained attention with a record on RCA called *Step to the Rear*. But Marilyn May was not all that good-looking and she was already in her thirties. Everybody was youth-oriented. So when I brought her around this time, all the agents at WMA said: "Spellman, you're crazy."

Nevertheless, I did sign Marilyn May.

There was always a sprinkling of guys in each department at WMA who had the same vision that I had, had the same "eye" that I had. They were the doers. One of them was a hot TV agent, Marty Litke, and he got Marilyn May on *The Kraft Music Hall*. One thing led to another, but the thing that really blew the lid off for Marilyn May was that she sang *The Star-Spangled Banner* at some sports affair and Alan Lerner of Lerner and Lowe fame called the WMA office to find out who Marilyn May was.

From then on, my career took on a life of its own, because agents who wanted to sign other clients would come to me to say, "Join me. I need your help on this." I became "the guy to go to" if you wanted someone to help make your client's career happen in a big way.

On April 30th, 1969, our first child was born.

In the delivery room the obstetrician pulled the baby's head out with the forceps.

Just as the baby's head was about to come out, the doctor stopped, and loudly asked, "Any bets?"

We all bet on our baby and we all won. We had a perfect baby. Cece's parents were delighted to have their first grandchild.

When it was time to bring Cece and our baby home from the hospital, Cece's parents grabbed the baby and took the child to our apartment in their car. It was like our baby was *their* kid! They were crazy about their first grandchild.

Of course, the arrival of a first-born in the Straci family solidified my relationship with Joe and Gigi-- Dad and Mom as they were to me now.

Then a little conflict happened.

I don't know where my mother-in-law got it. Maybe it was just wishful thinking on her part and she started believing what she wanted to believe. But I absolutely know that Cece and I never discussed religion with her parents as far as how we were going to bring up the kids. Gigi just presumed that we were going to bring up our kids as Catholics. Perhaps one of her rationales (which wasn't altogether wrong) was that in the Jewish religion, whatever the mother is, the kid is. So theoretically, our child was born Catholic; that is, if you wanted to be extreme in Jewish orthodoxy. But we never discussed any of this with Joe and Gigi Straci.

What Cece and I *did* decide about the religion was that I said, "We'll let God decide. If the first-born is a boy, then all of the kids will be Jewish. If the first-born is a girl, then all the kids will be Catholic."

And—- the first born was a *boy*!

Cece and I named him Matthew.

Shortly after Matthew was born, Cece and I sat down at the Straci dining table.

I said, "I never told you how we were going to raise our kids. *Now* I'm telling you how we decided."

Cece's parents accepted our decision. They were just thrilled to have a grandson at last! And years later, they both flew out to California to attend Matthew's bar mitzvah.

When Matthew had his bar mitzvah, I went through a conversion for my two kids. In Yiddish it is called a *mikvah*. The ceremony is somewhat similar to what is done in a Christian baptism where they dunk the kid's head into the water. *Mikvah* actually means "bathhouse," and that is where the ceremony is done, performed by a cantor. Present at our ceremony was the cantor, my two sons and a witness.

I felt that it was very important to have my sons go through this ceremony, to pass down my Jewish faith and heritage to them.

At the time of Matthew's birth, Jimmy Roselli's career was taking off, but Roselli was a hard man to work with. He was stubborn.

An example of how stubborn Roselli could be is how he almost walked off his first appearance on *The Ed Sullivan Show*.

Two things can kill a show business career: greed and ego. Why did Roselli want to walk off? Because of the marquee! It could only list a couple of names there outside the Ed Sullivan Theater at 52nd Street and Broadway. Sullivan, in the whole hour of his show, had a half dozen stars. He couldn't list them all. So Sullivan didn't have Roselli up there on the marquee.

Roselli said to me: "My name's not up there on the marquee outside!"

I said, "Who's going to see it on a Sunday night on Broadway? Four black hookers walking up and down the street? Meanwhile, on TV, sixty million people are going to see you around the country!" (This reminds me of a line Dangerfield once hit me with. I booked him in Florida to open for the Supremes. He said to me: "I don't know why you're sending me to Florida to be with the Supremes. I could stand on Broadway any given night and be with all the Supremes I want!")

In his book, Roselli always brought this

242

story up, saying that, "Spellman forced me to do Sullivan."

Forced him?

Despite Roselli, Roselli made a hit. His performance made television history. He started out with *Sorento* and killed the audience. He segued right into *Lull-a-bye of Broadway*. Roselli did a tribute to Al Jolson where he wound up on one knee, just like when Jolson did *Swanee*. The audience went to its feet. Ed Sullivan was astounded.

By the late 1960s Roselli was exploding big in New York, Pennsylvannia, New Jersey, Connecticut and the city of Boston.

I said to him, "Jimmy, let's have the rest of the country hear you sing. Okay?"

Roselli would turn away from me and shake his head when I would urge him to expand his territory of personal appearances. I couldn't understand it.

We could have made deals in major nightclubs in Pittsburgh and other points west.

When I went out to San Francisco, I spoke to the manager of a nightclub named Bimbo's. On that trip, I was servicing Al Martino who was appearing there. (Mr. Bimbo was quite a dresser; he even wore spats!) I pitched Mr. Bimbo on Roselli.

He said, "Okay. I'll try him. I can give Roselli fifteen hundred dollars a week."

I went back to Roselli and offered him the Bimbo's date. Roselli was already making $7,500 a week, which was pretty good for nightclubs.

Roselli asked, "How can I take fifteen hundred a week when I'm making seventy-five hundred a week in all these clubs back here?"

I said, "Yeah, but, Jimmy, we'll take short money in the beginning. You sing and they'll bring you back a second and third time! Each time they bring you back, I'll get you a raise! The money will come! But let's get you out there and let them see you first!"

Roselli wouldn't take the Bimbo's date. Thick, thick, thick!

Jimmy Roselli was very much localized in

his personal appearances, unfortunately-- for him. He could have been a big star I believe, but now he is largely forgotten by the public.

Buckalo should have pushed Roselli. But Buckalo had by now become such close friends with Roselli that he didn't want to pressure him to do anything he didn't really want to do. I used to go up to Amen's and plead with Buckalo to push Roselli to broaden his territory of personal appearances, but Buckalo wouldn't do it.

All Buckalo would say to me was, "If he doesn't want to do it, he doesn't want to do it."

Buckalo had a compassion for Jimmy, and maybe knew something about Roselli that I didn't. Maybe Buckalo had the key to what to me was the puzzle of Jimmy Roselli, the ambitious entertainer who didn't want to succeed.

Eventually Jimmy Roselli left WMA and booked individual dates on his own. His career faded. He was forgotten by the public. He was finally swallowed by obscurity.

Jimmy Roselli was a great talent, but he just

couldn't be made to understand what he needed to do in order to market himself to mainstream America.

Everybody is in show business.

If you're the butcher, the baker-- everybody has an opinion about something in showbiz.

I once co-produced a show called *Three from Brooklyn*. I got this racket guy who ran a chain of butcher stores as an investment backer for the show. The guy's nickname was "Tony the Butcher." He actually gave me a suitcase full of money, $50,000 in *cash*.

Now, Tony the Butcher was in show business.

Sitting in on a rehearsal for the show, all of a sudden Tony the Butcher starts saying, "Don't you think in the second act so-and-so ought to do this-and-that?"

All of a sudden Tony the Butcher is a director.

Everybody is in show business.

That attitude would prevail many times when you would take money from people to finance a show and they would have no background or knowledge about show business at all. But they all had something to say. They all became mavens.

In putting together a show, however, you take whatever you can get in the way of money. Sometimes it can be big chunks. One guy backing *Three from Brooklyn* put in $100,000. You want to try to get as big of chunks as possible, because you don't want too many partners. If you have more than 35 investors, you have to go through the Security and Exchange Commission, and that's laborious. If you have 35 investors, or less, you can go through the Attorney General, which is more expeditious. Now that Broadway musicals are costing so much money—- at least $10 million and upwards to $65 million-- the producers have to take as much money as they can from as many different sources as required. Even accounting for inflation, today the production of Broadway shows are much more expensive than they were in the twentieth century. Now advertising is very expensive. A full page ad in *The New York Times* is about $100,000. Also the unions have pushed for higher salaries and more for their pension funds.

Years ago, a performer did Broadway because it was a major event. Actors got paid about $2,500 a week. Now, if you really want a star, you're talking $20,000 to $50,000 a week. In the 1960s a strong headliner in a major nightclub could get $10,000 a week, and in Vegas top stars got something like $50,000 a week. I was able to get that first big Rock and Roll act I signed *Paul & Paula* $1,000 a night and the whole office couldn't believe that I was getting them such big money. It was unheard of for a Rock and Roll act to receive that kind of pay. Today, the same kind of artist with the same level of popularity would probably get $150,000 to $200,000 a night. Of course, ticket prices are going way out of whack. It's crazy.

By 1971, I had a name in the William Morris office in New York. Guys in the office were bringing me clients. Even my boss, Mr. Kalcheim, made me come with him to see some comic that I told him we should *not* sign. But he was very friendly with the comic's manager.

In the next departmental meeting, Mr. Kalcheim said, "Larry Spellman and I are going to sign so-and-so."

He wanted to use me as a criterion for judgment. If I okayed it, then you just had to know that Mr. Kalcheim knew what he was doing, too! I was being used to validate the judgment of Mr. Kalcheim-- my boss, one of the founders of William Morris!

But this time, I just couldn't take the "credit." I couldn't allow myself to be used in this way.

So I said, "Mr. Kalcheim, I think if you will recall, I said in the car that I didn't think that he had six solid minutes of television material."

"Never mind," Mr. Kalcheim replied. "I know you like him."

When the boss says you're right, you've got

to admit—-

you're right-- whether you like it or not.

This is the position I had reached in William Morris. Mr. Kalcheim was using me as his frame-of-reference, even though he was my boss.

To say that I was doing well at William Morris would be no self-serving exaggeration. Our annual Christmas party illustrated and underscored my success. There were two parties each year that, if you were invited, you were on the A-List: Lloyd Kolmer's New Year's Eve party and the Christmas Eve party that Cece and I gave every year at our apartment on Central Park South. Our Christmas Eve party was black tie. Jacqueline Suzanne, author of *Valley of the Dolls*, lived in our building, and she came to our Christmas party with her husband. This party highlighted my visibility and prominence at the office. It was the "in" office Christmas party for all the top agents at William Morris.

As I progressed in my career, I found that

difficult performers were the rule and that coping with their attitudes was all part of the business. It wasn't just Jimmy Roselli. There were a lot who were much worse than he was. Egocentric performers have no regard for anything. They would sell their mothers down the river for a nickel, if they could. Talk about ruthless!

One of the most egocentric performers I ever had the misfortune of doing business with was Joan Rivers. Her manager was Scott Shukat. Like me, he went to the High School for Performing Arts. Joan Rivers was a loner, because she was such an ugly girl. Scott was like a big brother to her. He would take her by the hand and they would go on the train together to travel to some little joint in the Village where she could try out new material. He ran with her, helped her, the whole nine yards.

When Scott Shukat left college, he came up and applied for a job at William Morris and got into the mailroom. I was already an agent at this time. Scott moved up out of the mailroom shortly and soon became an agent at WMA. He started doing very well for himself at William Morris, in fact, he started getting hot. At this time, Joan Rivers was managed by Jack Rollins, Woody Allen's manager. She was being represented by GAC, our competitor. Scott Shukat and I steal Joan Rivers away from GAC and sign her to William Morris.

Now Joan Rivers starts to get hot...and hotter....

Joan Rivers goes to Lee Stevens who was second in command at William Morris, and said, "I'm okay with Larry Spellman representing me. But I've got to have somebody more important than Scott Shukat."

Joan Rivers dumped Scott Shukat after he had been instrumental in signing her to William Morris-- Scott Shukat, her old manager, her old, devoted friend who had supported her, helped her and nurtured her when she was just an uncertain girl lost in the big, bad world. Joan dumped Scott like yesterday's trash.

Scott was destroyed.

Afterwards, Scott made a dartboard with Joan River's picture for the bull's eye. He used to throw darts at it. He was quite a marksman.

Then Joan River's ego set in. Think of how wet cement hardens. Her manager, Jack Rollins, couldn't take her anymore and he got rid of her.

And then I got rid of her.

We were having a conversation on the phone. It was going in circles. It was going crazy. Joan wouldn't stop with her impossible demands. I cut in on her with only two words:

"Get lost."

And I hung up on her.

I didn't need a dartboard.

But don't let me give you the idea that *all* showbiz performers are egomaniacs. There are always the few exceptions that help prove the rule. A couple comes readily to my mind.

The first was another woman performer. This lady was the exact opposite of Joan Rivers. She was the country-western singer Anne Murray, a very nice, sweet lady with great talent.

I was fortunate to be able to sign her to WMA and become her agent. The story of how I became Anne Murray's agent illustrates the surprises inherent in show business and how there is no precise formula for success.

I was up in Montreal at the World's Fair that they called "Man and His World." This fair was up there two years in a row. I had booked Peggy Lee there. I went to see her show and then all of us stayed at the promoter's house. Peggy Lee was with Capitol Records and the promotion men from Capitol Records were also staying there at the house with us. I got into a conversation with them.

One of the Capitol Record guys said, "You know, it's crazy, but you never know how things will turn out. There's a record happening on our label now, and we don't even know *how* it's happening, because we're not putting a quarter in promotions behind it. It's breaking out by the seams, getting major air time on the radio all across the country, shooting up the charts, hot as a pistol.

It's called *Snowbird* by Anne Murray. What a phenomenon! We don't have any idea how it's happening!"

This shows how you can put a ton of money behind something, but if the public doesn't want to buy it, they're not going to buy it. And here with something like Anne Murray's recording, you don't put a quarter behind it, and somehow it gets discovered.

I said, "Okay! Well, where is Anne Murray now?"

They said, "She's in Toronto."

So I flew to Toronto. I attended her performance at the Royal York Hotel. I saw how talented she was, how her record was taking off, and I signed her to WMA.

Right away we got Anne Murray multiple shots on Glen Campbell's TV show, and that, plus her record, sent her career into the skies and made her a star.

Then there was another performer I represented who, like Anne Murray, was a very nice person. He was a nice guy with a lot of talent. I'm talking about the singer Bobby Rydell.

I once booked Bobby Rydell at a club in Baltimore. I went down there for WMA to service his appearance and I took my long-time friend Stanley Solomon along with me.

Before the show, Stanley asked Bobby what his greatest gratification had been since he succeeded in show business.

Bobby Rydell replied, "Being able to buy my father a Cadillac."

So there were the two talented performers in show business I represented who thought about someone other than themselves all the time and were reasonable people. I wish I could think of more....

Oh, well.   Maybe they'll come to me...eventually.

Don't get me wrong. Show business is not all a grim, uphill battle with impossible personalities. Yes, I admit, it's really a hell of a lot of fun a lot of the time. It's just not the way most people think it is, looking at it from the outside in. It's a lot of illusion, a lot of smoke and mirrors. But sometimes the magic is comedic.

Comedian Jack E. Leonard was at our competitor, GAC. I was making a name for myself at WMA. Jack E.'s manager was dissatisfied with his client's representation at GAC, and so he told Jack E. about me and what I was doing at William Morris.

I had lunch with Jack E. Leonard at the fancy Toot Shor's restaurant. We talked about me representing him, but Jack E. sat on the fence. He was most decidedly undecided. I felt this was a case where I could get the prospective client to decide to sign if I had a lot of time to keep talking, keep pitching, to keep, well, keeping on until I wore down his vital reserves, until exhaustion forced him to finally say, "All right, already!"

I knew that Jack E. was going to play the Venus Club in the suburbs of Baltimore. The club was one of my accounts. I used to go there all the time, so I used it as an excuse.

I said, "Jack E., I've got to see those guys who own the thing. Don't fly. I'm going to drive down. Come on down with me."

I wanted to nail his agreement to sign with me in the car. Jack E. was no dummy, so I'm sure he knew right off why I made him this offer. But he took my up on it. Maybe he wanted to see what I could do with my pitch. Maybe he just wanted to make me earn my commission. But he agreed to ride down to Baltimore with me.

So I had Jack E. Leonard there in the car with me for the four hour drive down to Baltimore. In the four hours I listened to Jack E.'s stories and he listened to my pitches. We went back and forth. Everything he said, every story he told, was only an introduction, an illustration of my following pitch about why he should sign with William Morris. I sold soft. I sold hard. I sold endlessly. I could see that Jack E.'s vital reserves were being exhausted. He was losing his will power to say, "No."

By the time we got to Baltimore, to the

Holiday Inn next to the Venus Club, Jack E.'s reserves were all gone.

"All right, already!" he sighed.

"Does that mean you're going to sign?" I asked.

"Yes! Yes!" he said. "I told you twenty minutes ago!"

"I didn't hear," I said.

"You were talking," Jack E. said. "Here's the place. Let's go in!"

So we went into the coffee shop at the Holiday Inn, sat down and placed our orders. Although Jack E. Leonard had done some television, he was not so well known to the general public. He was basically a nightclub comedian. The waitress recognized Jack E. because he had played the Venus Club so many times before. Jack E. and the waitress chatted briefly, and then she went away.

In a few minutes, the waitress came back, and said, "Mr. Leonard, there's a long-distance call for you."

Jack E. got up and went to the phone. He came back in thirty seconds.

I said, "That's the quickest long-distance call I ever heard."

Jack E. said, "It was an independent agent from California. He said, 'Jack! I hear you're leaving GAC.' And I said, 'Well, I'm thinking of going with the William Morris office.' And the agent said, 'No use spending any more money on this long-distance call.' And he hung up."

There are definitely some light moments in show business that keep us happy-- and keep us young!

One time the football star Joe Namath came up to my office at WMA with Anne-Margaret, her husband Roger Smith and Alan Carr, the producer of *Grease*. They came to talk to me about a project on which Anne-Margaret was working at the time. So during this meeting I became acquainted with Joe Namath.

That year at the Super Bowl the Jets were going to play the Baltimore Colts. Baltimore was my territory. That's where I booked the Venus Club, such as I had done with Jack E. Leonard. So I used to go down to Baltimore a lot. I would stay there at the Holiday Inn, which was only a block or so away from the Venus Club. The Baltimore Colts used to go there to the Holiday Inn to drink. Back then in their heyday the Colts had Johnny Unitas as their quarterback. So before the Super Bowl, I met all of these players in the Colts there at the Holiday Inn, and we were talking about the big game. They said that they didn't even think that the Jets belonged in the same ballpark with them. That's how they thought the Super Bowl was going to be-- a joke, a pushover.

So afterwards, I was in the elevator at the William Morris office. It was just Joe Namath and me in the elevator alone, riding down.

I said, "Joe, I've got to tell you something. The Colts just told me that they don't think the Jets even belong in the same ballpark with them.

They're saying the Jets are losers, pushovers."

Joe Namath replied, "Larry, bet on me. Bet on me. I tell ya, I know how to beat 'em."

The Jets were a 16 point underdog.

Sure enough, later I'm at a friend's house in Queens along with a lot of other guys. We were all there to watch the Super Bowl. I told them that the Jets were going to win. I offered to take everyone's bets. They all thought I was crazy.

The Jets?

I said, "Whatever you want, I'll take the bet."

I took their bets. They all laughed and said I was going to lose my shirt.

Joe Namath beat the Colts outright. He made history.

Joe Namath was truly a Broadway character. Everyone called him "Broadway Joe." He would show up at the Copa on Saturday, drinking until 12 o'clock at night, and then go out and play a football game the next day.

Joe Namath came in to the Copa one time

wearing a full-length fur coat—- a *guy* wearing a *fur coat*! And a football player, no less!

But guess what?

The next day, all of us guys who had seen him there at the Copa in his fur coat all ran out and bought full-length fur coats of our own! *I* bought a *fur coat*! I can't believe I did, but I did. I bought a fur coat and *wore it in public*. I wasn't ashamed. We all were sporting fur coats! All of us, walking around in fur coats! It was a thing. But Joe Namath started it. We're lucky he didn't start something else!

Joe tried a little acting. He appeared in a movie or two. I saw him in Atlantic City where he put on a show called *Sugar*, a take-off on the movie *Some Like It Hot*. He wasn't any good at all. He just couldn't act. But so what?

Joe Namath was a great football player.

He was unbelievable.

Sports have always been a big part of my life. I was never really a player, but I've always been a big fan. And fans *have* to see the game.

It was 1970, opening night at the Plaza Hotel. This was one of the chicest premieres in New York City. This opening night Monday was black tie. For the premiere, I had booked the singer Carol Lawrence who had starred on Broadway in *West Side Story* and who was married to Robert Goulet. She was a big name and a big talent.

However, that same Monday night was a premier football game that, perceptibly, was going to be bigger than any Super Bowl. It was the Minnesota Vikings playing against the Baltimore Colts with Johnny Unitas. The Viking's defense, "The Purple Gang," was considered unbeatable. They used to win games for the team, not their offense. This was a game that no real fan could miss. You just *had* to see it!

Yet, the opening night at the Plaza Hotel was a major show business event, and if you were in show business in New York, you just *had* to see *it*!

What was a sports fan in show business going to do? Be in two places at the same time?

All of us sports fans in show business, and there were a lot us, were faced with the same dilemma. That Plaza Hotel opening night just could not be missed; it was a very big event. Danny Thomas, Dick Shawn, everybody in town was there at the Plaza. Sol Shapiro and Lee Salomon were there, representing WMA. Cece and I were there.

Harry Rome, Carol Lawrence's manager, was a big, big gambler. He would bet $500 on a football game. Arthur Dooley, the manager of the Plaza Hotel, was also a big football freak. All the guys, Lee Salomon, myself-- we said, "What the hell are we going to do? We're going to miss the big game!"

Well, I had an idea.

I showed up with a small Panasonic TV set with a little pop-up screen and a little ear plug for the sound, and I put this little TV under our table, plugged in the ear plug, turned on the set, and tuned in the game.

I had the game on, watching the action underneath our table.

Nobody knew a thing about what I was doing with the exception of the most die-hard football freaks who sat around and behind me, crazy to know the action on the field. But only I could see the action, playing out at my feet, right underneath the tablecloth parted before me.

So while Carol Lawrence was up there on stage doing her act, *I was watching the game and listening to the announcer with the sound plug in my ear*!

And all the guys sitting around me—- all of them rabid football freaks-- were asking me:

"What's happening now?"

"What's going on now?"

"What's the play?"

"What's the score?"

Meanwhile, Carol Lawrence had absolutely no clue as to what was going on down below her, what we football freaks were doing. She was singing up there, and we guys were down below keeping score! She was belting her heart and soul out, and she would look down and see us enthralled and elated-- *at the game*! She would look over at us, give us a wink, and we would go wild with ecstasy—- because...*there was another touchdown*! Yes! Yes! Yes! Carol just knew she was hot! She just knew she had us in the palm of her hand. Every time the audience would applaud, I would give all the guys around me the latest news on the game! The applause would drown out my voice. We got it down to a system.

All the guys couldn't believe that I would have the audacity to do something like that. But when you're a real fan, you just *have* to see the game.

It was a great night for show business and for sports, a double premiere. And, as far as I know, Carol Lawrence never found out what we did. Sorry, Carol. I think she would understand.

This was how it was in those days. They were exciting times. Then *The Godfather* motion picture project got under way, and I became involved with trying to get the singer Al Martino a part in the movie. That's a story all in itself.

CHAPTER TEN

Making An Offer That Can't Be Refused

As the late 1960s drew to a close, I represented the singer Al Martino. Like Jimmy Roselli, Al Martino had some mob connections. But to understand those connections, you need to know a little more mob history.

Let's go back to the early part of the twentieth century. In those days the mob was known as "The Black Hand." It was run by old Sicilians who were called "Mustaches." The young guys like Vito Genovese, Lucky Luciano, Joe Straci, Joe Columbo, Joe Profaccio and Joe "Bananas" all felt that the "Mustaches" were in the way, so they waged a campaign of killing all these old guys. The young Italian guys used the Jewish mob to do the assassinations for them. The old "Mustaches" always protected themselves with bodyguards all the time, knowing each day could be their last. The old "Mustaches" didn't recognize the guys in the Jewish mob. So the Jewish guys would come in disguise under some pretext. Some of the Jewish hit-men would dress like cops. Once the Jewish guys got inside to the "Mustaches," they would wipe them out. They would do this anywhere, at any time. They kept this going through Prohibition, until the last of the "Mustaches" were dead.

Then Prohibition ended, the Depression set in, and the mob settled down somewhat to doing things in a more negotiating manner. In the 1940s, Albert Anastasia was a big mob boss who ran the longshoreman's union. He was eventually assassinated by the mob while sitting in a barber's chair.

Anastasia's nephew by marriage, Tony Scotto, was put in to the presidency of the union. He was the real-life counterpart of the character that Lee J. Cobb played in *On the Waterfront*. Vito Genovese was one of the five partners running the

East Harlem mob with Lucky Luciano, Frank Costello, Frank Lavorse and Joe Straci. Lucky Luciano was the titular head of all the five families. It was Genovese who got to FDR, and said, "If you don't want disruption and labor strife on the docks, you've got to let Lucky Luciano out of prison." And the government did let Luciano out, and after World War II they exiled him to Italy.

Lucky Luciano, in order to have civility and order in the mob and no more killings, formed the Syndicate, and ran it like a corporation. Before anybody had to be "eradicated," it would have to be discussed amongst the Syndicate's commission. They had to reach the decision of whether or not a guy could be "rubbed out." They actually had a group of killers controlled jointly by the Jewish guy, Louie Lepke, and the Italian guy, Albert Anastasia. This eventually became a business to itself, "Murder Incorporated." It was murder by contract. If you were just "Joe Citizen," you could get rid of your partner, and you would pay these guys money to do the assassination. This business took on a life of its own beyond just executing the orders of the commission. There was a big market to serve the needs of people who wanted to "bump off" a friend, relative, spouse, neighbor, or business partner. Up until then, this market had been overlooked.

Albert Anastasia got to be too outlandish for the tastes of his associates. He started to evince anti-Semitism. He was rubbing Meyer Lansky the wrong way. Meyer Lansky made money for all these guys. He was the financial genius among them all. Anastasia, Luciano, Bugsy Segal and Lansky all grew up together as kids. They were all East Side kids, all friends. They grew up and became top Mafia guys, and Lansky made the money for them. Luciano and Segal were the muscle.

But Anastasia became too much of a sore point in Meyer Lansky's eyes. So they got Anastasia right in the Park Sheraton barbershop while he was in the chair, getting a shave. In broad daylight a guy came in and pumped several bullets into Anastasia's head. Anastasia had let his bodyguard run errands. It sounds like a set-up that everyone knew was set-up, except for Anastasia.

The guy who ran a little Jewish mob in Bensonhurst, Brooklyn was named Abe Rellis. He was a kind of sub-contractor for Louie Lepke, his "mechanic." He would take assignments to go out and do the killings. When it came to Jewish hits, Rellis would do them. The Jewish guys who grew up as criminals were just as tough as the Italians.

Now, here is where the mob influence penetrated to the courtroom system, even to the judges.

They finally got Abe Rellis to turn state's evidence. To protect him as a witness before the trial, they hid him out on Coney Island in a dumpy hotel called The Half-Moon. This was a high-rise building, and they put Rellis in a room several stories up from street level. In the room with Rellis they had four detectives stationed. The detectives were there to guard Rellis, to see that he remained safe from all attack. So there sat Rellis, safe, secure, beyond all possible reach.

Next thing you know-- Abe Rellis went out the window!

They found him below on the sidewalk, dead.

The cops said, "He must've jumped when we weren't looking."

Yeah, that would explain it.

Four cops in the room and they all turn and look away from Rellis at exactly the same instant, and, because the cops looked away, Abe Rellis saw his great opportunity and immediately took a swan dive out the window, hoping he'd find a trampoline.

Everybody knew it was a joke. The Mafia got to the cops. They must've paid them a ton of money. The cops threw Abe Rellis out the window. That shows the mob's power.

Why did Rellis have to go? He and Lepke were bringing too much "heat," taking murder contracts left and right, carrying them out too sloppily, too publicly. His superiors felt Rellis had no finesse. And Lepke's associates felt that Lepke lacked proper judgment. All this sloppiness in a string of highly visible murders drew the attention of no less than J. Edgar Hoover. J. Edgar Hoover felt that he had to do something about Lepke, because Hoover was starting to look bad while all these murders were going on. Hoover was looking to arrest Lepke, but Lepke hid out.

The mob went to Lepke and said, "Look, Louie, you're bringing too much heat on us. We've made a deal with Hoover. You will do X amount of years, and then you'll get out. You'll be okay."

Lepke agreed to the deal that the mob had cut with Hoover. They arranged for newspaperman Walter Winchell to bring Lepke by hand to meet J. Edgar Hoover. Winchell got Lepke in the car and they drove to the prison. They tried Lepke, found him guilty of mass murder, and electrocuted him in the electric chair.

There never had been a deal with Hoover. The mob double-crossed Lepke.

The mob had talked Lepke into giving himself up, but they knew what was really going to happen. It was all a set-up. But there was so much "heat," the mob felt they had to do it. The mob couldn't pay off guys like J. Edgar Hoover. This shows the limits of the mob's power. The "heat" that Lepke was generating was going to jeopardize all of the mob's businesses, legitimate and illegal. They didn't want Big Law down their neck. Individual cops, they could pay off, but not the F.B.I., not I.R.S. guys.

Back in the 1950s, Al Martino used Albert Anastasia to back his career, and, of course, he had that hit record called *Here in My Heart*. Albert Anastasia got Al Martino into all the big nightclubs.

Then, all of a sudden, Al Martino didn't want Albert Anastasia anymore. Martino felt Anastasia wanted too much of his money. So Martino told Anastasia, "Good bye." Anastasia sent Martino a telegram with just two more words:

"Good luck."

Right after that, two guys nailed Martino in an alley in Atlantic City. One guy held Martino while the other guy worked on Martino's face with a knife. He cut Martino up badly.

Martino had to go to England to live and work there for seven years until he was able to work his way back over here to America. A friend of the family talked to Angelo Bruno, head of the Philadelphia mob where Martino was from, and Martino was allowed to come home. Years later in the territorial battles between the Philadelphia mob and the New York City syndicate for control of Atlantic City, Bruno was assassinated and peace was made between the two factions. This all happened before I ever knew Al Martino, before I was even an agent.

Then, about 1965, I signed Al Martino with William Morris.

Of course, the big story in regard to Al Martino and the Mafia was the making of the movie version of *The Godfather*.

At first, for the part of the singer "Johnny Fontaine" the producers of *The Godfather* wanted

Frank Sinatra, but the mob told Sinatra to turn it down. Mario Puzo, the author of *The Godfather*, had used Sinatra as the real-life basis for the Fontaine character. Sinatra resented the fictional parallels with his own life. In particular, he hated the incident in the novel involving the horse's head which was pure fiction. It was Sinatra's position that he got his part in *From Here to Eternity* purely on the basis of doing a good screen test. Sinatra had confronted and yelled at Puzo in Chasen's restaurant, and Puzo had walked out. So there was no question of Sinatra being in the movie version of *The Godfather*.

Then the makers of *The Godfather* went to Vic Damone, and Sinatra told Damone: "You'd better not do it."

Al Martino wanted to do the Fontaine part in the worst way. Francis Ford Coppola didn't want Martino. Interestingly, Paramount didn't even want Coppola. They didn't think he had the ability to write and direct it. Martino later told me that they were writing the screenplay as they were filming it.

278

The screenplay wasn't even finished. They were just writing it as they were going along.

How did Al Martino finally get the part of "Johnny Fontaine"?

Al Ruddy, the producer of *The Godfather*, was an inveterate gambler and he owed $75,000 in markers in Las Vegas. He couldn't pay.

Martino found out about this, and told Ruddy: "I'll pick up your markers. You get me into the movie."

So Al Martino gets the offer to be in *The Godfather*, and all because Al Ruddy got an offer that he just couldn't refuse.

But then Russ Buffalino, a big mob boss from the Scranton area, came to New York. He used to hang out at a famous Italian restaurant called Vesuvio's.

Martino came running into my office one day, and said, "I just came from Vesuvio's. Russ Buffalino-- he told me I can't do *The Godfather*."

I said, "You go back and tell Russ Buffalino that your agent is Larry Spellman whose father-in-law is 'Joe Stretch,' and you're doing the movie."

And then Russ Buffalino and I became very friendly.

Then Buffalino had a singer that he brought to me, a kid from Italy that United Artists records was going to use to take Jimmy Roselli's place (because Roselli was breaking the chops of United Artists, too). Danny DiMino wrote songs for the kid.

Danny DiMino spent ten years in prison because he wouldn't squeal on things that he knew. But DiMino was a talented song writer who wrote Dean Martin's hit *Return to Me*. He wrote that song in prison and Frank Costello got Dean Martin to record it.

The mob controlled all the jukeboxes. I met the guy in charge of this business one time down in Florida, a guy named Al Minniacci. If a Frank Costello told a Dean Martin to record a song, you can bet that a Dean Martin was going to record it. Then-- when they *made* the song a hit is when they got the recording of it into all the jukeboxes of

America. It was all interconnected. That's how things happened.

When *The Godfather* was being cast, it was the hottest thing going. You couldn't go to a party without people asking, "Who is going to play Don Corleone? Who's going to play Sonny?"
So if you were an actor, and you landed one of these leading roles, it was unbelievable.

An actor named Carmine Caredi landed the part of "Sonny" which James Caan eventually played. Do I have to tell you that Caredi was on Cloud Nine?

I'll never forget Caredi coming up to the dressing room at the Copa to see Jimmy Roselli. Of course, the whole mob was in there with Jimmy. They were all excited, saying, "Carmine is going to play Sonny! We can't believe it!"

It was very exciting for everyone there.

But then Marlon Brando told Coppola: "Caredi is too old to play my son. Get somebody else."

And that's how James Caan got the part.

Caan was slimmer and lighter, Caredi was a heavyweight, so he looked older.

After Carmine Caredi lost the part, he became a drunk. It destroyed him.

One funny thing about *The Godfather* was how the mob was so opposed to it at first, but then later really got into it and almost became fans. What turned it around was when Joe Columbo gave Al Ruddy the go ahead to do the movie. Some of the mob guys were even on the set when they were filming on location in Little Italy. Although some of the mob guys criticized details in the movie, such as the kind of hat Brando wore, *The Godfather* was generally accepted as being an authentic fictional depiction of the American Mafia.

Later, when they made Godfather II, Coppola called me and said, "I want Martino again."

Martino had gotten practically no money at all for the first movie. But he got tremendous mileage out of his part. He did make a lot of money in personal appearances after he did the movie. So now it comes to the second *Godfather* movie, and Coppola offers Martino the same thing he paid before.

I said, "Come on! You've made millions on the first movie. And now you're offering him the same thing? Are you out of your mind? You're insulting. Why don't you get Jimmy Roselli?"

And I hung up on him.

So Martino didn't do the second *Godfather* movie.

Martino wound up doing *Godfather III*. I was not managing him at that time.

I got this story from Owen Laster at William Morris who made the deal for the film rights to *The Godfather*.

Mario Puzo was broke, feeding a family. His book came out, and before it became a hit, he said to Laster: "If you can make a motion picture deal for me, make it."

Puzo only got $50,000 for the screen rights to *The Godfather*. The picture made multi-millions. They did go back to Paramount, and Paramount graciously added to Puzo's pot, but nothing compared to what it would have been if Puzo had held out for more at the beginning. But he didn't dare, because he was so broke.

In reading *The Godfather* you knew that it was a compilation of different characters, real-life characters, but Puzo fictionalized it. Like Brando's character "Corleone" was the Olive Oil King. Well, in real-life that was a guy named Joe Prafaccio. So all the stories are intermingled, based on true events and true characters, but Puzo changed everything around. Like, Joe Straci was not assassinated. But now in *Godfather III*, they were in Atlantic City having a conclave, and just before the helicopter came down, shooting everybody, Pacino says: "I tried to get out of the Mafia, but they won't let me out. They drag me back in." He says that, "So-and-so won't let me out and *Straci* won't let me out."

So Joe Straci, my father-in-law, was mentioned in the *Godfather* movies, but it was just fiction.

That is, until life imitated art-- and Joe

"Stretch" Straci-- was kidnapped!

CHAPTER ELEVEN

The Law Becomes Independent

Something happened in the early 1970s to Joe Straci that was similar to an incident in The Godfather.

In the movie version of *The Godfather* a rival mob tried to assassinate Marlon Brando's character, Don Corleone, while he was buying fruit. When my father-in-law went to the garment center, he would usually walk around the corner from 58th Street to 59th Street between First and Second Avenues where his car was garaged. One morning as he was walking there, he got kidnapped. Those who kidnapped him wanted to talk to him about conspiring with them to overthrow another mob organization. If he wouldn't have acceded to their plans, they would have probably killed him.

Two guys surrounded Joe Straci as he was

walking on First Avenue. They got him into a car stopped at the curb. The driver of the car then took off.

As the driver turned on to the ramp of the 59th Street bridge, Joe Straci saw his one chance to stay alive. He suddenly elbowed the guy next to him, reached over to the door handle and twisted it open with a single jerk. The door flew open. The driver hit his brakes. The car swerved. Its tires squealed.

Inside the car, Joe Straci was fighting for his life. He had pushed his way over the top of the man seated next to him, swinging his elbow out hard into the man's chin.

Then Joe Straci leapt through the open car door.

He hit the pavement, rolled down an incline, and came to a stop down in a gutter.

People standing on the street had seen Joe Straci jump out of the car. There were too many witnesses. The kidnappers sped away on to the bridge.

Joe Straci got himself home. If he knew anything, he knew how to survive.

I got a call at the office to come over to the Straci townhouse right away.

When I got over there, I saw twelve guys with guns sitting around the dining room table. The one and only time I ever saw Buckalo at the Straci house was right then. He was there having a private conversation with Joe Straci.

My father-in-law was stretched out on the sofa. Buckalo was in a chair sitting next to him, talking. Buckalo wanted to know all the details of what had happened so he could find out who these guys were that had just kidnapped my father-in-law.

Joe Straci was all bruised and cut up. He had been bandaged around his knees and elbows. The fall when he had hit the pavement had been very hard.

"Dad," I asked, "what's happened to you?"

"Some guys grabbed me," my father-in-law said. "We're handling it. It's all over with. Nothing to worry about."

The guys with the guns continued to stay around the dining room. They stayed for days, guarding my father-in-law. At night, when most of them went home, they would open the front door and slowly and carefully look left and right as they exited. Each and every guy in sequence would do exactly the same thing, like soldiers trained for war. And that's what they were, and what they called each other—- "soldiers."

My father-in-law in later years never had a bodyguard, so he was vulnerable to an attack like this. Actually, they were never called "bodyguards." They were "drivers." My father-in-law once told me that years earlier there had been a rivalry between the East Harlem mob and Dutch Schultz's mob over the unions, a conflict about who was going to dominate. My father-in-law thought Dutch Schultz was crazy and would do just about anything. He told me that he always had to have my mother-in-law, Gigi, accompanied by a bodyguard.

The guys like Joe Straci were heads and

shoulders above the likes of Dutch Schultz. That's why Joe Straci was successful in developing relationships with major politicians, judges and the upper echelon of the police department. He dealt with people in a diplomatic, businesslike way and was a master of the art of strategic compromise.

Buckalo and his partner Fat Tony were the titular heads of the East Harlem mob, because my father-in-law no longer did the day-to-day things. Fat Tony grew up in the organization being my father-in-law's driver. Fat Tony was the money interest behind the opening of Caesar's Palace in Las Vegas. I got meetings set up for me at Caesar's Palace because of Fat Tony. Rudolph Guiliani made a name for himself as a prosecutor when he arrested Fat Tony in the middle of the night, taking him to jail in his pajamas. One of Buckalo's underlings turned state's evidence, a guy known as "Joe Fish." Fat Tony never came out of prison.

Buckalo dropped dead one day of a heart attack in the early 1970s while he was walking along a pier on City Island. He was heavy, over-ate and he smoked. I was not surprised when I heard of his death.

My work at William Morris was so prominently noticed amongst the Mafia guys.

One day in the early 1970s I got a collect call from a guy. He was calling me from a prison in Atlanta, Georgia. Ordinarily, I would never pick up a collect call. It was sort of anti-office policy to do so. When I heard the name of who was on the line and that he was calling me from a federal prison, I had to take the call. I picked up the phone.

The guy said, "I heard all about you. I want to know if you could bring some talent down here to entertain the prisoners."

This underscored the fact that *my name was out there*.

I knew I was big in Atlanta, Georgia...amongst the Mafia guys, anyway. All the Mafia guys in New York who got convicted of federal crimes ended up in Atlanta. That was the location of the East Coast Federal Penitentiary.

Before I came out to California, my father-in-law introduced me to "Jimmy Blue Eyes." He was the "Italian messenger boy." That is how they depicted his fictional counterpart in *The Godfather* movie, Hyman Roth's "Italian messenger." Jimmy Blue Eyes was that to Meyer Lansky. He was the conduit between Meyer Lansky and the Italians.

Jimmy Blue Eyes had sent an ex-convict named Dino Conte out to California to get into the movie business. I was introduced to Dino Conte by Jimmy Blue Eyes when we all met with my father-in-law on the street corner of 58th Street and First Avenue. Obviously, my father-in-law got Jimmy Blue Eyes to instruct Dino to watch out for me while I was in California. Dino Conte was the producer of all the early Conan the Barbarian movies starring Arnold Schwarzenegger. Dino Conte got hot all on his own then. He produced the movie *48 Hours* starring Eddie Murphy.

My years at William Morris had been good. March of 1972 rolled around. It was a Don Rickles opening at the Copa. This was when Don was at the height of his career. He was white-hot, his timing razor sharp, going for the jugular. The place was packed.

A girl singer named Karen Wyman was starting to gain some attention. We all thought she was going to be the next Eydie Gormé. We had booked her to open for Rickles to give her some exposure. So I invited an ex-agent, Irvin Arthur, to see Karen at Rickles' opening. Irvin Arthur was dying to go, because it was something to get in to see Rickles at that time. Everybody wanted to see Rickles.

At my table was Irvin, my brother-in-law, Ron Straci, and Russ Buffalino.

Into the Copa walks "Crazy" Joe Gallo. You wouldn't call him "Crazy" to his face, but that was his reputation. Gallo had his own little mob in Redhook, Brooklyn, which was a real tough neighborhood. Crazy Joe walks in with his group of guys.

Irvin Arthur recognizes Crazy Joe. He turns

to me and asks, "What did you get me into?"

I said, "What do you think you're in-- a movie or something?"

The problem was that right before this in Columbus Circle on Italian-American Day the mob assassinated the head of one of the big families in Brooklyn, none other than Joe Columbo. They shot him down right in Columbus Circle. Everyone attributed this assassination to Crazy Joe Gallo. So everyone knew that the Colombo mob was out to get Gallo.

Carmine (who was the head of the black-coated maître d's at the Copa) knew that Gallo was coming into the club. Carmine told me that he was packing two guns because he knew what might happen once Gallo got there. If the Columbo guys could ever "pigeon-hole" Crazy Joe, they were going to kill him.

Crazy Joe Gallo comes right up to our table, and Irving says: "Well, yeah, but..."

"Come on," I said. "Nothing's going to happen. You're in the Copa."

The show goes on. Karen sings. Rickles kills—- with laughs, not bullets. The show finishes. It's peace in the valley. We all go upstairs to the lounge. We go to the bar. Irving goes home. Guess he had his fill of all the peace.

So it's just Ron, Russ Buffalino and me there at the bar.

Suddenly, Crazy Joe and his gang come clambering into the lounge, escorted by Carmine with his two concealed weapons and a couple of other of the Copa "black coats" who also were probably "carrying." Everything's nice. Carmine takes this crowd toward a table in the corner of the lounge so that Gallo had to pass the three of us standing at the bar. Gallo recognized Buffalino, and he comes over to us and starts chatting with Russ.

Gallo said, "You know, today is my birthday. After this, we're all going down to Little Italy to get some squngielles at Vincent's. How about coming with us?"

We all said, "No thanks. We appreciate it, but no thanks."

We didn't go.

Seven o'clock the next morning the phone rings. In New York, if you get a call at seven in the morning, you know somebody has just died. This time, it was Irvin Arthur on the line.

Irving said, "I told ya! I told ya! I told ya!"

I said, "Irving, what the hell are you talking about? It's seven o'clock in the morning!"

Irving replied, "I know exactly what time it is, and boy do I hope I woke you from a sound sleep! It's on the radio, all over the radio!"

I asked, "What's on the radio?"

"What I told ya," Irving said. "I told ya it was going to happen and I'll be damned if it didn't happen!"

I asked, "What happened?"

Irving said, "What happened? The hit, that's what happened! The hit happened! Right down there in Little Italy at Vincent's last night! A couple of Columbo's guys came in, spotted Crazy Joe Gallo, and they called up their cohorts and they all came over and gunned down Crazy Joe. Killed him dead. Shot him full of holes! Larry! It was a bloodbath, I tell ya! A bloodbath! If we would have been there, we would have been caught in the crossfire! We would've been shot full of holes too! Larry! Are you hearing me? Did you hear what I just said?"

"Yeah," I said. "I'm hearing you."

"Do you understand what happened?" Irving asked.

"Yeah, yeah," I said. "I understand. It's...it's terrible."

"Yeah, it's terrible," Irving said. "I tried to tell you. I tried to tell all of you guys!"

"I know," I said. "You tried to tell us. You were right."

There was a pause on Irving's end, and then he asked:

"Where did you guys go after I left?"

It took a second for me to reply:

"Home."

Sam Giancana was one of the most famous

Mafia bosses in history. Giancana was Al Capone's successor. Today, most people know Giancana as the guy who backed Frank Sinatra.

From his home in Forest Park, Illinois, it is said that Giancana ordered the "elimination" of over two hundred men. Some of these guys were just shot, but a lot of them were tortured to death on meat hooks and with blowtorches, baseball bats and electric cattle prods. You didn't want to get Giancana mad with you.

Giancana had business interests all over the U.S., Mexico and down in Central and South America. He was loaded with dough.

Giancana's girlfriend was the singer Phyllis McGuire of the McGuire Sisters. Phyllis McGuire was a socialite and friends with Kirk Kerkorian. She was always attending society events and getting her name in the papers. This put Sam Giancana's name and face in the papers as well when he attended these events along with her. So there was a lot of "heat" on Sam Giancana.

Giancana came to the Copa to see Jimmy

Roselli in his dressing room. Giancana had a gorgeous watch worth $40,000. He took it off and gave it to Jimmy.

But the New York "guys" didn't want Giancana around because he was as hot as a pistol with the Feds. He had an F.B.I. agent assigned to tail him everywhere he went. So Giancana brought a lot of attention, a lot of "heat" everywhere he went. The "guys" just didn't want all that attention directed at them.

My father-in-law met with Giancana, and told him, "You're carrying too much heat."

So Sam Giancana left the country. It made all the newspapers: "Sam Giancana in Mexico." It was my father-in-law who pushed him out.

One by one these mob guys dropped out of the scene. They either were pushed, shot, tripped, fell, heart attacked or—- like Hoffa—- disappeared into the Beyond. Time marches on for everybody, even old "soldiers" who don't necessarily always fade away, despite whatever MacArthur said about it.

January 1972 my second son, Chris, was born. Once again, Cece delivered a perfect baby.

As Chris grew, it was clear that he was very precocious. At the age of two he had a full vocabulary. Chris was the exact opposite of his brother.

Matthew talked gibberish up until he was almost five years old. This situation scared the heck out of Cece and me. We took Matthew to all kinds of child psychologists, trying to figure out what the problem was. They finally diagnosed it. They said that Matthew's mind was working faster than his ability to execute verbally what was on his mind. So he was just blurting out whatever *he* believed was language. He thought he was talking. Thank God that, not only did he change, but he became so loquacious that if you would ask Matthew what time it was, he'd tell you how to build a clock!

Opposite to all this, Chris had his full vocabulary at the age of two.

We moved to One Lincoln Plaza right after Chris was born. We needed another bedroom. Chris was so hyper he would run into everything. At two years of age he had a double hernia. Chris was just a wild, rambunctious kid, bursting with energy. We ran him over to the hospital so much to have him checked for minor injuries that the staff there got to know Chris on a first-name basis.

Matthew and Chris were close as brothers and got along very well. They were always talking to each other.

My relationship with my wife, Cece, couldn't have been better. How can I say it? Life with Cece was the life I had always dreamed of, always wanted. And now I had it. Cece was an extraordinary woman. Everyone loved her. If you had known her, you would have loved her. Here is something that once happened that illustrates the kind of person Cece was.

One time we were at a very famous Mexican restaurant called El Parador, a major hang-out where agents and models would come. We-- Mel

Marx, his date, Cece and me-- were sitting in a booth, having dinner. In the booth next to us, a girl got up and started heading to the bathroom. Cece immediately picked herself up and started following her.

When Cece came back, she said, "I saw when she was heading to the bathroom that she looked green and sickly. Sure enough, she was and I helped her throw up."

This sick girl was a perfect stranger. But that was Cece. She only knew how to give, not take.

Cece was an absolutely devoted daughter. When we moved to California, she called her mother and father every day. She was always doing little things for Matthew and Chris and me. And boy was she a great cook! How could any man ever want a better wife? How could any child want a better mother?

It was great just to come home from the office and be with Cece and our two sons. It was so normal. It was so good. It was so *real*.

If you're getting the picture of a very happy time in our family life, you're getting the right picture. We went on a lot of family car trips, and crisscrossed the country half a dozen times. We never made a reservation anywhere. We just enjoyed the open road. If I saw a billboard that I liked, I'd say, "Let's go. I want to take a look at that." Cece and the kids had things they wanted to see, too. It was always an adventure. Sometimes we would get stuck with the two kids, the dog and the station wagon with no motel in sight. We would pull up to a rest stop, pull out the blankets, and stay the night. When we would wake up in the morning, we'd see 14 other cars out there with people sleeping inside of them just like we were doing in ours. There was camaraderie. It was fun being on the road. Any family who lived in the 1960s and 70s and traveled the highways knows what my family and I experienced. We were just being Americans. These were very, very good times for us.

However, in a career sometimes, especially

in show business, good times can be a warning that rough times are ahead. That was what I began to realize at the office in early 1972, just after Chris was born. I was at the apex of my career with William Morris. But I was getting antsy. I was looking at guys who had left William Morris and had made a big success out of themselves, guys like David Geffen and Bernie Brillstein. They had the temerity to leave the protective umbrella of William Morris and take their shot at doing business all on their own. I admired that temerity, that courage, and I started planning on doing what they had done. I wanted to take my shot.

At this time in early 1972, Nat Kalcheim had already retired. Lee Stevens was second in command at William Morris. He took me to lunch, and we had a long talk about my future.

I didn't tell him I was leaving the agency, I only told him about my discontent with the job. They really wanted me to stay with WMA. The comptroller, a guy named Larry Lewis, said, "You've got to be crazy. They all think you're going to be the next big executive around here."

It wasn't that I didn't want that. It was that I knew the immediate future was going to be frustrating. Nat Kalcheim was an icon. Good, bad or indifferent, you had to give him the highest respect. Working for him was fascinating. His second in command who took over, Sol Shapiro, was a statesman also. He did a lot of foreign business. He read *The Wall Street Journal* every day. You could have an adult conversation with him. After they moved Sol Shapiro out, Lee Salomon took over as the next boss. He was a hot-shot nightclub salesman, a typical "sweetheart, chicky-baby" type of showbiz guy with initials here, initials there. I respected his sales ability, but I didn't like his style, his personality. Nobody really liked his personality. I was going to have to answer to Lee Salomon. I was only 36. Salomon was in his late 40s.

So I talked to Lee Stevens about the possibility of transferring me to another department or out to California.

Stevens said, "No, between you and Lee Salomon we have the best nightclub department going. We really want you here."

I asked, "Then is this going to be it for the rest of umpty-some years?"

I started looking again at guys like Geffin, Brillstein, Jerry Weintraub and Irwin Winkler who eventually produced the *Rocky* movies. They all took their shot.

So I said, "I'm going to take my shot."

That's the reason I left.

I went to Lee Stevens and told him my decision.

He said, "I want you to take ten days off and think about it."

Cece and I planned to take the family on a car trip to the Shenandoah Valley. The night before we had planned to leave, there was extreme flooding, rain, storms.

I said, "Cece, we can't drive down there. We'd have to be crazy."

I called my brother who was working at that

306

time as a travel packager.

I said, "Talk to your partner and see if you can get us on a plane to Acapulco."

And that night we were on a plane to Acapulco. Cece, the two kids and I had a great ten days there. All I did the whole time was lie on the beach in the sun, looking up at the sky, and thinking: Should I or shouldn't I leave WMA?

After all that deliberating, at the end of the ten days I still had reached no decision.

When we got back to New York, it was my father-in-law who made the decision for me.

He said, "Look, Larry, you could weigh this, you could talk about that. But the bottom line is: Are you happy? Or are you unhappy? If you're unhappy-- go."

So, go I did.

I went and told Lee Stevens I had made my decision.

I told him: "I'm leaving William Morris."

Once you tell them you're going, they want you *out*. I told them on a Wednesday. They told me to be out by Friday. However, they didn't exactly boot me out, either.

Today show business is cold-hearted. But back then when I left WMA there was a feeling of family solidarity. William Morris gave me the money that was due me as far as profit sharing, but they also gave me my vacation money *and* they gave me my *Christmas bonus*! Keep in mind that this was *July*.

It wasn't like I was leaving to go to another agency. In that case, they would have made me leave the very second I told them I was resigning. That would have been because they didn't want you taking your files with you. Giving information to a competitor was considered horrendous, but opening up a personal management business as I was now planning to do was another matter entirely. Here, I would be acquiring clients that, hopefully, I would be bringing *to* WMA for representation. We had the potential of a continuing business relationship.

I *did* take my big Rolodex with me. Shortly afterwards,

I got a telegram from the office. They wanted the Rolodex.

They said: "It's our property."

I knew what they wanted. I found out.

Lee Salomon had said to them: "He knows night clubs in places all around that we don't know. That's how he books all those clients of his. That's what keeps him going. He *found* places we never knew existed. It's all in his Rolodex. We've got to get that back!"

So what I did, I took out of the Rolodex all the things I wanted to keep, such as the nightclub contacts. I left the Rolodex cards with all the numbers for things like...my uncle, my brother, my tailor, that kind of thing.

The office sent me a telegram asking for the rest of the numbers.

Then Lee Salomon called me, and said, "You've got to be kidding."

I said, "I sent you the Rolodex. That's what you asked for."

My departure from William Morris made

front page of weekly *Variety*.

I formed a personal management company with Irv Siders and Herb Paloff. We opened an office on 48th Street and Madison Avenue. Herb was very big in the lounge business. Irv had a lot of contacts and knowledge. In his heyday he had managed Phyllis Diller and Vaughn Monroe. Except for Herb's lounge business though, we didn't have any clients. I had walked out of WMA thinking: Boy, I hang out a shingle and the business is going to come to me. This is going to be it!

But without my connection to WMA, I found that doing business was very hard. People who returned my phone calls when I was a William Morris agent now no longer returned them.

We gave the company a try for three months. Marvin Shnayer called the shot.

He said, "You'll never last with Irv Siders."

Irv Siders was a manager. I was feeding him clients. He was a buddy. I was at his house in West Hampton on weekends and all that. But then his real personality came out, and I saw that his well-known reputation for being gruff and irascible was well-founded. It was hard to work with him and live with him. So, after three months, I left.

I then became involved with a management company called Complex IV. Its headquarters was in Connecticut. At first, I was commuting to Connecticut one day a week. Then it was two days, three days a week. We got busy. We grew by leaps and bounds. I was eventually up there five days a week.

I finally said to Cece: "We've got to move up there to Connecticut."

We got an expansive apartment on the ninth floor of a gorgeous high-rise in a beautiful section of Bridgeport, Connecticut. It was actually two apartments. We knocked down a dividing wall to make them one apartment and we gave the kids the master bedroom.

We had been living there in Bridgeport for about six months when my nephew, Mark Spellman, came to visit. This was August 1975.

311

It was the height of the summer heat, but my son, Chris, age 3, put on his new, heavy cowboy outfit that he had received as a present so that he could show it to his cousin. Although he was sweltering in his get-up, he was thrilled all the same. The outfit was all heavy garments from head to toe-- and thank God that it was!

Cece, Mark and I were in the dining room, having brunch. My son, Matthew, who was *not* a jokester, came in from their bedroom where he and Chris had been playing. Matthew's face was white as a sheet and his mouth was wide open.

"Chris went out the window," Matthew said.

"What are you talking about?" I asked, rising from my chair.

"Chris just went out the window, Dad," Matthew repeated.

I couldn't believe my ears. I ran back to the bedroom. I saw the open window. The screen was out. My stomach tightened. It couldn't be. It was impossible. I lurched forward toward the blue sky and looked down through the window at the ground nine stories below, not knowing what I was about to see.

And I saw Chris.

He was down there.

He had fallen. God help him, he had fallen.

CHAPTER TWELVE

The Other Coast Explodes

"Daddy! Daddy! Get me out of here!"

It was Chris. He was calling me. He was alive. His little figure lay far below, sprawled in a bush.

I spun around and ran toward the front door.

"Call 911!" I shouted as I ran out.

All I had on were my briefs and bathrobe. Instinctively I ran down the hallway toward the stairwell, passing the elevator. I ran down the stairs, down all nine floors to the ground, and out of the building. I heard Chris. He was still calling out to me from where he lay in the bush. I ran to him and gently lifted him out of the tangle of limbs and leaves. I got him out of the bush and wrapped him in my bathrobe. Although it was summer and Chris was heavily clad, his skin was cold and white, and his eyelids fluttered. I held Chris in my arms and started running.

Felix, our doorman, came running around the corner. Having been conditioned in New York to have to wait for an ambulance to get through traffic, I wasn't about to wait for help.

I yelled to Felix: "Get your car! We've got to get to the hospital!"

Just as I got Chris into Felix's car, sure enough I hear the wail of sirens. It sounded like they were coming from all over. There must have been something like sixteen official cars plus an ambulance.

But I said, "Felix, don't stop."

Felix hit the gas and we kept going at top speed, no stopping for lights, no stopping for nothing.

I kept talking to Chris, "Don't fall asleep. Don't fall asleep. Don't fall asleep."

Chris kept fluttering his eyes. I knew he was going out. I knew we had no time.

When we pulled up to the hospital, a whole

army of nurses and doctors were waiting outside at the emergency entrance. Felix came to a stop beside them, and I opened the car door. The nurses took Chris, still wrapped in my bathrobe. I got out of Felix's car and followed them inside, wearing nothing but my briefs.

We got inside and they took Chris into an examining room. I sat down on the floor in the outside hallway. And that's when I fell apart. I started crying like a baby.

Then the nurses came out. They handed me my robe and I dropped it across my knees.

"Mr. Spellman," one of the nurses said. She knelt down beside me. I tried to look at her through my tears.

"Your son is going to be all right," she said.

"Chris?" I asked, not believing.

"He's conscious," the nurse said. "His vital signs are stable."

"He fell," I blurted out, "nine stories."

"We know," the nurse said. "They told us."

"He's not injured?" I asked.

"The doctors are examining him," the nurse said. "We'll be doing tests. But just keep in mind that your son is young, and kids his age are very resilient. Is someone coming for you?"

"My wife and nephew," I said.

The nurse looked at my robe.

"You should put that on," she said. "You're going to get cold out in this hall."

The nurse stood up. I started putting on the robe. All of the nurses started to turn away.

"Nurse," I said.

The nurse that had been talking to me turned around.

"Thanks," I said.

She nodded and then turned to the others and they all went back into the examining room.

Cece, Matthew and my nephew, Mark, soon showed up at the hospital, and I told them what little I knew. They had brought me some clothes and I put them on. We waited a long time and then a doctor came out. He sat down with us.

"Good news," the doctor said. "All the tests

have come back and Chris is in very good shape for a little boy who has just fallen nine stories. The whole thing amounts to a broken leg and a black eye."

"That's it?" I asked. "No internal injuries?"

"There are no indications of internal injuries," the doctor said. "Of course, we'll be watching him. He's going to have to stay here awhile. We're going to put his leg in traction."

"Can we see him?" Cece asked.

"In a little while," the doctor said. "We're going to a put a cast on his leg."

Later, we all went into the room and saw Chris. He had the shiner, all right, and his leg was up in a cast. But he didn't look as bad as I thought he would.

"Chris," I asked, "how do you feel?"

"Bad," Chris said.

"What happened?" I asked. "How did you fall?"

"Superman," Chris whispered, and closed his eyes.

"I think he needs to rest now," the nurse said.

We all left the room.

Outside in the hall, I asked Matthew: "What did he mean by 'Superman'?"

"We were playing Superman," Matthew said. "We were jumping off the table, pretending to fly. Chris tried to jump off the table, but he slipped, and fell backwards. He hit the screen, and went right through the window."

Cece and I looked at each other as Matthew told this.

"My God," Cece said.

"He's going to be all right," I said.

My nephew Mark said, "Sounds like Chris was Superman, after all."

"He's just a very lucky little boy," Cece said. "I should have been watching him better."

"You can't watch Chris twenty-four hours a day," I said. "We had no reason to expect that anything like this would happen."

I had to agree with Mark. It did seem like

Chris was super. Whoever heard of anyone surviving a fall out of a nine story window? Somebody ought to have called Guinness. Somebody *did* call a lot of other people. The nine story fall Chris had taken suddenly became worldwide news. As we were walking through the hospital, we were told that news about Chris was being broadcast all over the radio and television.

I immediately went to a phone and called Cece's parents. My father-in-law had already suffered a bit of a heart problem, and I didn't want him hit with a shock by hearing the story about Chris secondhand. I knew that Cece's parents were at a wedding, but not exactly where. I made a whole round of calls, and finally was able to track them down and reach them at the wedding. I was hoping that I could get my mother-in-law on the phone to break the news to her so that she could ease it to my father-in-law.

Instead, I got my father-in-law on the line first.

I said, "Hi Dad. How're you doing?"

I just didn't know how to tell him.

Joe Straci said, "How am I doing? I'm at a wedding, that's how I'm doing. I'm busy. What is it?"

I said, "Well, I..."

"Come on," he said. "You're calling at somebody's wedding."

I realized there was no way to tell him, but to tell him.

"Chris is fine, Dad, "I said, "but he fell out the window of our apartment. But don't worry he's fine."

"What do you mean, 'Chris is fine'?" Joe Straci asked. "Your apartment is nine floors up. Are you telling me he fell out a window way up there and he's not hurt?"

"He broke his leg, I said, "that's all. Just his leg. The doctors say he'll be all right."

"What did he hit?" Joe Straci asked. "What did he land on?"

"A bush," I said.

"Where was the bush?" Joe Straci asked.

"On the ground," I said.

"Nine floors down?" Joe Straci asked.

"Yes" I said. "But they did tests and Chris doesn't have any internal injuries. He's going to be all right."

I heard Gigi's voice in the background. I could hear Joe Straci talking to her, "Now, Gigi, don't get nervous and don't get excited. I've got to tell you something, all right?"

I was worried about my father-in-law's reaction. But instead *he* was worried about my mother-in-law's reaction. Both of them took the news a lot better than I thought they would. It hadn't occurred to me that they had both lived long lives and had weathered many storms in their time.

I couldn't get hold of my brother-in-law, Ron, right away. He was on his boat. He had it docked over on City Island. We got hold of the harbor police and sent a boat around to tell him what had happened to Chris.

We just barely got the word out to our family members before news about Chris was all over the place.

Television crews from ABC News came up from New York and interviewed me. Stories about Chris made newspapers all around the world, in Germany, in England. Priests and nuns came to see Chris.

I said to them: "He's really Jewish."

They replied, "We don't care. It's a miracle."

Everybody had their take, their own explanation of how Chris had survived his nine story fall.

A professor from the University of Michigan came to our apartment and interviewed us, and studied the trajectory of the fall that Chris took out the window. The next thing I knew, the professor had an article in the newspaper, describing the flight Chris took, complete with an illustration of our apartment showing the trajectory of the fall with a series of arrows.

Two police detectives came to our apartment to look at the window where Chris fell, just to make sure that no foul play was involved.

Everybody had a theory, an idea, or explanation about how it all happened.

All I can say is that the cowboy outfit that Chris had put on that day had padded and protected him. Also, the bush upon which Chris landed had prickly leaves that held him in place and cushioned his fall. The flight trajectory that Chris had taken out the window was so unique that it took him right into that thorny bush. Right behind the bush was a set of outdoor light fixtures, the tops of which were spiked, similar to the spikes on old, Prussian army helmets. In front of the bush was an expanse of solid concrete. It was an extreme long-shot that Chris wound up in that bush. He could just as well have fallen upon those spikes atop the light fixtures or upon the concrete sidewalk. In either case, he would certainly have been killed. But he fell into the bush! And he fell into it wearing that thickly padded cowboy outfit. My explanation? It was another example of "The Hands of Fate."

Right after Chris went into the hospital, a

friend of ours, Ron Yatter, a TV packaging agent with WMA, took our son Matthew to stay with him and his wife, Marsha, for a couple of weeks. They were great with Matthew, and it allowed Cece and me to concentrate on taking care of Chris. We had to do a lot of driving back and forth between home and the hospital. That alone really ate up our time. And we spent a lot of time at the hospital comforting Chris who was only three, as well as consulting with the doctors and nurses. We were worried about him at first, but before long it started becoming clear that Chris would be all right.

On one of our visits to the hospital, we took my father-in-law to see Chris. As were driving away from the hospital after our visit, a cop car passed us, made a U-turn, and put on his siren. I pulled over and stopped, thinking: What did I do?

The cop got out, came up to my car window, and asked, "You're Christopher Spellman's father, aren't you?"

I said, "Yes."

He said, "I was on my way to the hospital. I

have a gift for the kid. We all talked about it. A bunch of us pulled up at the same time when it happened, state troopers, sheriffs. We didn't know what to expect. We thought we might have to pick up pieces from the concrete."

The cop handed me the gift.

"Thanks," I said.

"My pleasure," the cop said, and he went back to his car.

Through this whole crisis Cece was calm. She was calm when it happened and calm afterwards at the hospital. She was very strong in that way. Cece understood the vicissitudes of life. But looking back, perhaps it was here after Chris took the fall that Cece became very protective of Chris, even babying him.

After Chris returned from the hospital, he was none the worse for his experience. We all put it behind us, and our lives went on.

Matthew, in those days, was a bit of a roly-poly. He was very good with a knife and fork. He had a habit. He used to enjoy his food so much that, when he would eat, he would hum: "Mmm-mmm-mmm! This is delicious." It was cute as hell. Matthew applied himself in school. He and his whole generation throughout those years were good kids.

When Matthew was around twelve or thirteen years old he shot up tall, and he decided all on his own that he wanted to put himself into real good physical condition. He was tired of being a roly-poly. He started reading books on physical development. He read Schwarzenegger's book on body building. He started working out with weights and doing exercises. Soon Matthew became a physical specimen. Years later, Matthew and I attended a black-tie affair at the Friars Club and Schwarzenegger was there. I introduced Matthew to him. Schwarzenegger was a very nice man. He spent fifteen minutes talking with Matthew.

After Matthew graduated college, he was still into body building and wanted to be an actor.

I said to him: "I want you to follow your

dream. You go to New York, because that's where you're really going to learn."

The theatre world is in New York. If you really want to do theatre, you have to be on the New York scene as a New York stage actor.

Matthew was never lazy. He was always willing to work and be self-supporting. And because he was physically what he was, he went around to different apartment buildings in New York handing out flyers about his services as a physical trainer. Doing this, he built up a clientele as a private trainer.

Then one of his clients told him about one of his friends, Jeff, who ran a very prominent boutique Wall Street-type of firm on Madison Avenue. The firm traded options for major clients. Matthew interviewed for this firm, and they hired him. He became a physical trainer for their company. The guys in the company were all "young turks" who believed in "healthy bodies, healthy minds." Matthew was with the company many years working as their physical trainer. They loved him.

Matthew, by osmosis, caught the bug of Wall Street trading. He used to go down to the office at 5 o'clock in the morning, trained these guys before the market opened, and then, while the market was open, he headed back home and did his own trading on the computer. That's what he's doing now and he's doing exceptionally well.

Matthew came up with a formula of how to marry an active company with a dormant company. He brought this formula to the firm and they used it on one deal and made a ton of money. The point is: Matthew wanted to be an actor, and look how "left field" he went. Life takes a turn. We have to go where life take us.

In March 1974 I went out to Los Angeles on a business trip representing my company, Complex IV. I took Cece and our two kids along with me. The last part of my trip I was supposed to see the buyer of entertainment for the Fairmont Hotel chain in San Francisco. The Fairmonts at that time all had showrooms playing stars. I was going to sell some things to them. I called the buyer to reconfirm our meeting, and she cancelled on me.

So I said to Cece: "You know it's a Wednesday afternoon in March. If we get back home, we'll be too tired to run up to Vermont for a quick weekend of skiing. We can't swim in March. Ever see Palm Springs?"

Cece said, "No."

I said, "Neither have I. And all the hot-shots keep talking about Palm Springs. You want to go?"

We checked out of the hotel, rented a car that Wednesday night, drove down to Palm Springs, checked into a little motel, woke up Thursday morning-- and got into the pool with the two kids.

We were all swimming under clear, blue skies in the middle of March.

I said, "How long has this been going on?"

It was ninety degrees, no humidity. The skyline of mountains was still snow-capped. I thought we were in Shangri-La!

I said, "I can't believe this. I've got to get a piece of this!"

I bought a home in Palm Springs the very next day.

Buying the home was the catalyst that eventually led to us moving to California, because after we bought the house, I immediately asked, "Now how are we going to use this?"

It took me two years to shift my business from back east to California.

In March of 1977 I broke up with Complex IV. I set up my own management company, Larry Spellman Enterprises. We took an apartment in Beverly Hills for one reason and one reason only: so we'd have the weekends in Palm Springs. If that buyer for the Fairmont chain hadn't cancelled our meeting, I would have never moved permanently to California!

Over the next several years I conducted my management business out of our apartment in Beverly Hills with Cece working as my secretary. For a while during this period I had a separate office in Beverly Hills.

Jackie Mason left the representation of Joe

331

Scandore and became my first client. I had met Jackie Mason years earlier when he became a client at William Morris. Mason had appeared at Arturo Cano's The Boulevard, and I took my brother and his wife to see him. So when I left Complex IV, Mason came to me and said that he wanted to go with me and my new management company. Then I got Pat Cooper, Al Martino, Kathy Lee Crosby, Laine Kazan and Sal Richards.

One of my clients was Ralna English who was part of the husband and wife singing duo "Guy and Ralna." Ralna and her husband, Guy Hovis, were regulars on *The Lawrence Welk Show*. Ralna wanted to prove that she was more than just a Lawrence Welk singer. She wanted to sing jazz.

There was a restaurant/club/lounge next to NBC Studios in Burbank named Chadney's. I took the then associate producer of *The Merv Griffin Show* out to Chadney's and we had dinner. We were going to walk into the lounge to hear Ralna sing jazz. She was performing alone, without her husband, Guy.

John, Merv's associate producer, asked me: "Who are some of your other clients?"

So I told him my list.

He asked, "What do you do? Walk around with a bottle of aspirins all day?"

John had a very good idea of what I was up against with many of my clients.

I was trying to push all the clients on my list when I heard about what Joey Bishop was doing. He was supposedly retired on a fortune that he had put into real estate. But I heard that he was working in a "joint" in Wildwood, New Jersey, and that he had been playing there for ten straight weeks!

I said to Cece: "He can't be doing this for no reason. I bet he's itching to get back into show business and he's trying to see what he can do."

We flew to New Jersey to meet Joey Bishop and see him perform. We already knew Joey because he was a member of the Englewood Country Club where my in-laws were members. Joey Bishop was friendly with Joe and Gigi Straci there at the country club. A lot of show business personalities played golf there. My father-in-law played golf there.

Cece and I went to Wildwood, New Jersey (a poor man's Atlantic City) to see Joey Bishop do his act at a place called "Crazy Morley's."

I said to Cece: "It's one thing to get up and have some fun one night, but he's doing ten weeks. He's trying out to see how he's doing. He's honing his act. He's anxious to get back to work."

We watched Joey's act, and he was very good, very sharp. After the show, I spoke to Joey in the back of the room.

I said, "I know you're dying to go back to work. You wouldn't just be doing this for fun."

Joey said, "Well, I'm not marketable. I don't think they want me anymore."

Don't forget that Joey Bishop had been a major headliner and a member of Sinatra's Rat Pack. In the 1960s, he had been the star of his own TV situation comedy and a talk show. He had made a ton of money. He had signed a new contract with ABC for his talk show, but a few months into the contract, ABC cancelled his show. Merv Griffin had started his own late-night show. With both Merv Griffin and Johnny Carson doing late-night talk shows, Bishop just couldn't hold on to his audience. When word came that his show was being cancelled, Joey Bishop walked off the set of his show right in the middle of taping. Vic Damone, who was scheduled to go on as a guest, encountered Joey Bishop and his wife going down the hallway on their way out of the studio.

"Where are you going?" Vic Damone asked him.

"We're going home," Joey Bishop said. "They cancelled me, so I'm leaving."

"Right in the middle of the show?" Vic Damone asked. "This is unbelievable!"

Well, if you knew Joey Bishop, as I came to know him, it *was* believable. It was a perfect example of his irascible character.

Joey Bishop had a smart accountant/lawyer put all his money into real estate. He owned all that block of office buildings on Robinson and La

Cienaga in Beverly Hills. He was collecting all those rents. In the 1970s, Joey did a few roles in movies and on occasion substituted for Johnny Carson on *The Tonight Show*, but for all real intents and purposes, Joey Bishop was retired.

The fact that Joey Bishop walked off his own TV show in the middle of taping it should give you a small clue that he was not an easy guy to work with. I've had a lot of show business clients in my day, people like Frank Gorshin, Kathy Lee Crosby, Sid Caesar, and every one of them had their idiosyncrasies. They all had their "crazies." You could see it coming, especially when you had to tell them something they didn't want to hear. With Gorshin—- if you've ever seen that bit from an Abbott and Costello movie: "Slowly he turns...." And then the guy would go ballistic. Sometimes almost anything could set one of these people off. Like:

"Hey, nice sweater you're wearing there."

"What do you mean by that?"

"Nothing. I just thought..."

"Are you insinuating there's something wrong with it?"

"No, not at all. I..."

"Watch it! Watch it, you."

"Watch what?"

"Your insults. Watch it with your insults. I won't put up with them!"

"I wasn't..."

"Don't deny it!"

Just typical showbiz pleasantries, just small talk from the Big People. So it was the same with Joey Bishop. You would simply be talking to him and he would suddenly turn on you.

Then why did I take all this?

Simple. These stars with all their "crazies" *were the best at what they did in the whole world.* They were brilliant in their talent. And I was a glutton for talent. I respected talent. I worshipped talent. It was the driving force behind my whole career in show business.

And if you want to talk about talent, nobody in my lifetime, and I handled a lot of comedians, nobody was as fast with ad-libs as Joey Bishop. He didn't use four-letter words. He never took cheap shots to get a laugh. His humor was all the real stuff based upon surprise, incongruities and timing. He had a brilliant mind. He exercised his mind, not by doing crosswords, no. He would get books where he would have to *break the code*. That's how he'd do his mental gymnastics.

Joey Bishop told me: "You think I'm fast? Groucho is the fastest."

I told Joey: "I can get your career going again."

So Joey Bishop took me on as his manager.

One of the things I got Joey involved with was in touring his act in a variety show format. The variety show played all over the country at places like schools and Masonic temples.

Joey Bishop's variety show was promoted by a guy named Roy Radin. Radin was a show promoter and also involved in the motion picture business. He raised money to help produce the movie *The Cotton Club* starring Richard Gere. He raised the money through the Florida drug traffic. Roy was a guy who would "double-talk," that is: *lie*. This created problems for him, because things have a way of coming out in the final analysis. He must have made certain people promises of this, that, and the other. *The Cotton Club* did not make money. Radin couldn't pay back his money people, so they (it is assumed) killed him. His body was found dumped in Malibu Canyon.

But before all this happened, Radin promoted Joey Bishop's variety show. Yes, I knew Roy. Radin would rent different venues in various towns and then go to the local police or fire department, and ask, "You want to help me sell tickets? I'll give you ten percent." Ostensibly, it would be a benefit-type show for the police or fire department. These local departments would then go to the merchants in town and get them to purchase blocks of tickets.

I got into a major beef with Roy Radin in Cleveland, Ohio. We were there at a high school auditorium where Joey Bishop was scheduled to do his variety show. Standing in the hallway outside the entrance to the auditorium was Radin, his bodyguard, a member of the dance team who was Joey's old friend and me. Roy Radin had not paid us for this venue, and I had reached a point with his "double-talk" where I no longer trusted him.

I told Radin: "We're not going on unless you pay us."

Radin shouted, "Whaddaya mean? Joey's doing his show!"

I said, "No, he's not."

Radin made a little move. The next thing I knew his bodyguard lunged at me and punched me in my face.

I went back against the wall, and then down.

CHAPTER THIRTEEN

The Law Is Tested

My back started sliding down the wall, the strength in my legs going out, my face shattered with pain. I struggled to remain conscious.

Radin's bodyguard had sucker-punched me. He was moving in toward me with his fist swinging downward for a second time.

Suddenly the guy on the dance team grabbed hold of Radin's bodyguard and held him back. Several people came out into the hall.

The dance team guy said to them: "Call the police."

With all the people standing around, Radin's bodyguard backed off. In minutes the cops came and grabbed the bodyguard. I was taken to the hospital. Roy begged me not to file charges.

When I got out of the hospital, Radin and I

met in the hotel suite and he paid us off for the show. I let the thing with his bodyguard go and didn't file charges. I went back home.

I'm in Beverly Hills. A phone call comes in. It's Roy Radin, asking us to play a date for him in Pittsburgh.

I said, "No way. I'm not going through that again."

Radin didn't tell me, but while he was talking to me on the phone, he had a guy he called "Uncle" on the line listening in on our conversation. This guy wasn't Radin's real blood-uncle, but a guy who was mob-connected. When I said "no" to us doing the Pittsburgh date, "Uncle" suddenly interrupted me.

"Uncle" said: "You're going to play the date."

I said, "No, I'm not."

"Uncle" asked: "Do you know who I am?"

I asked, "Do you know who my father-in-law is?"

"Uncle" said, "No. Who?"

342

I said, "Joe Stretch."

The line went silent.

Finally "Uncle" said, "Well, then, we had better talk about it."

I had to fly back to New York with Joey Bishop, and he and I had to have a "sit-down" at an Italian restaurant on Mulberry Street in Little Italy. Joey and I went in with two Mafia guys, one of whom I knew and was very friendly with, a guy named "Frankie Flowers." That was his nickname because, ostensibly, he was in the flower business. He too was a victim of the territorial war. They shot him while he was on a Philadelphia street corner standing next to his daughter. She was not hurt but they did this in order to send a message that you are never safe if you're a marked man. Roy Radin was also there with his "Uncle," an old-timer.

At the "sit-down" Radin's "Uncle" was quite humble. But Joey Bishop was very humble, also. I've always said that these guys like Joey Bishop, who said and did outlandish things at times, were people you had to excuse because of their

343

artistic temperaments. They just couldn't control their emotions. They were like children. But watching Joey at this "sit-down" I thought: if he's sitting in front of some big Mafia guy, would he act the way he does with me when he's doing a show? He didn't act that way at the "sit-down." He knew how to keep a lid on his temper there. He knew how to control himself there. Joey Bishop knew how to be humble at that meeting. He knew how to mind his p's and q's. So when performers sometimes act like jerks, it's because they know they can get away with it. They have a little power, and they use it, or, I should say, misuse it, because they become their own worst enemy.

The discussion with Radin and his "Uncle" proceeded calmly, quietly, civilly. A lot of inconsistencies came out in Radin's story as the conversation progressed. There were a lot of things that Radin had never told his "Uncle". Radin had been "double talking"—- even to his "Uncle"! Radin hadn't been playing straight with anybody. That was Roy: half-truths. The old-timer looked around and realized he couldn't make any of Radin's demands stick.

In the final analysis, we didn't play that Pittsburgh date. I was not surprised when I later heard that Roy Radin had been murdered. When a guy plays games with the mob, they play for keeps.

Here's a perfect example of how you can work your guts out in the personal management business, but the talent you're working for has no appreciation for your effort. Comedians love to make jokes about their agents, but what their audiences don't know is that many times, for an agent, show business is a game played on a one-way street with a sign that reads: "Do Not Pass Go. Do Not Collect $200."

Starting from the git-go with Joey Bishop, I said, "I can get you going. I can get your career rolling again."

He said, "Listen, you're not going to be able to get me going as a headliner, because those days are over."

But, at that time, in Las Vegas, opening acts were getting big, big money. This was because the hotels believed that if an opening act could bring in two hundred people on their own (coupled with a headliner) they would be worth a lot. David Brenner was making $40,000 a week as an opening act for Joan Rivers.

So Bishop said, "They're using David Brenner. They're using Pat Cooper. So if they get *me* as a second banana-- they're going to love it!"

So I took a meeting with a hot new agency that was really happening called Regency Artists. They had Johnny Mathis and Henry Mancini. They had a lot of good names. But they were hungry, too. I told them the game plan.

They said, "You sure Bishop is going to take second banana?"

I said, "Yeah. It's his idea."

Joey Bishop came up with a strategy.

"Brenner's getting forty thousand?" he asked. "We'll take thirty-five."

Well, these guys at Regency Artists couldn't

believe it.

"Are you sure he'll do that?" they asked me.

"Yeah," I said.

Regency Artists took out a full page ad in all the trades. They booked Joey Bishop over-night into the Aladdin in Las Vegas. He was to open for Freda Payne who had the hit record *Band of Gold*. She was a hot singer at that time. They also booked him with another hot new singer named Jane Oliver up in Harrah's at Lake Tahoe. We got booked suddenly with $300,000 in dates.

Some of the buyers, like Doug Bushauser, called me, and asked, "Are you sure Bishop is going to open?"

I said, "Yeah, sure. He's all set."

Things were going very good. I even got luckier now.

The big, hot Broadway show *Sugar Babies*, starring Mickey Rooney, had been playing for about a year. Mickey Rooney wanted to take some time off from the show. I was able to get Joey Bishop to be Mickey Rooney's first replacement for four weeks.

I flew to New York to meet the producer of *Sugar Babies*, and I made the deal for Joey Bishop. I got Joey the same money they were paying Mickey Rooney.

I'll never forget this. Joey Bishop is on Broadway, starring in *Sugar Babies*. His name is up on the theatre's marquee in bright lights. Joey, his girlfriend and I are at a delicatessen on Broadway and Seventh Avenue. (Joey was a big ladies man, and he had a girlfriend from Philadelphia with him, even though he had been married a long, long time.)

Joey said to me, "Larry, I can't believe it. I had a TV show. I had a talk show. I headlined by myself at the Sands in Vegas. But now I'm on Broadway. My first time on Broadway! My name is billed *above the title*! *On Broadway*!"

Joey looked over at his girlfriend, and then back to me, and said, "I can't open."

I asked, "What? What do you mean?"

"In Vegas," Joey said. "I can't play Vegas

as an opening act."

"What are you talking about?" I exclaimed. "Why can't you?"

"Because I'm *not* an opening act," Joey said. "I'm a headliner! I'm a Broadway headliner!"

And with that Joey Bishop cancelled all the second banana dates I had booked for him! Dates for very big money, the kind of money a headliner would love to get! The reality was that they *were* headliner dates, even though he wasn't getting top billing. If he had played those dates, he could have moved up to headliner billing very quickly. But his mind was made up. He had "made it" on Broadway and now he "had to" headline!

Well, can you believe the flak I got when Joey Bishop cancelled those dates?

At the Aladdin was a tough, ex-New York bookmaker named Ed Torres who was mob-connected.

Ed said, "I got all the billboards up. I got all the signs up. Joey Bishop at the Aladdin! Joey Bishop coming to the Aladdin! I got the word out to the high-rollers. I got everything going!"

Ed's voice dropped a register in rage as he added quietly, "If it wasn't for you and your family...I'd kill this bastard."

I had booked about $300,000 in dates that Joey Bishop cancelled.

Doug Bushauser came back at me now with the: "I told ya, I told ya, I told ya!"

About two years later I booked a show called *That's Italian*. One of the cast members of the show was Dean Martin's daughter. When I told her I had managed Joey Bishop, a look of disdain spread across her face. You could imagine all the stories she must've gotten from her father about Joey Bishop.

Joey rubbed a lot of people the wrong way.

The agency had to take out all their ads about his appearances.

Joey Bishop did this all along. He would get you started, get you worked up, you'd think you had a big deal set up for him and then he would come up with the stupidest excuses to cop out of it.

Eventually, after five years of putting up with this kind of behavior from Joey, I just couldn't take him anymore.

The bottom line is: If you're not making money with it, forget it.

I looked at my W-9 at the end of the year and I said, "That's all I made from him? I can't take this aggravation. He's not worth it."

I called Joey and said, "We've got to part ways."

I was representing Jackie Mason in 1977 when he got cute. I put him in the original MGM in Las Vegas, a place where he had not been able to get in before I put him there. He was a big hit. But then, Mason tried to welch on his commissions to me.

He had a girl working for him that acted as his assistant. They had a love affair. He used her. Mason's girlfriend would fight the Ethiopian army for him. She was a tough cookie.

I found out Mason wasn't paying anybody.

351

Mason put up money to produce his own movie. He welched on the director. He owed a lot of people.

Mason was playing Dangerfield's. I went to see Rodney's partner who, by the way, used to be the bass player at Danny Segal's The Living Room. His name was Tony Bevacqua.

I said, "Tony, before you pay Mason his money, he owes me a lot of money."

And Tony pulled out a drawer of legal notices and judgments of all the people that Mason was screwing and to whom he owed money.

So I got hold of a couple of Mafia guys that I knew. Apparently Mason had a friend who was connected to a mob in Brooklyn. I had to fly to New York to have a "sit-down." It happened in a bar in Brooklyn. Jackie Mason wasn't there, only his envoy who was mob connected from the garment center. At that time my father-in-law was getting sickly. I didn't want to bother him and get him involved with this. So I had to try to do this "sit-down" on my own.

So Mason's envoy was there. Two of my guys were there, me and the guy who "held court," who rendered the decision. I told them what Mason owed me, but, to tell the truth, without the backbone of my father-in-law, I wasn't too successful in pressing my case.

I saw the meeting was going the wrong way, so I said, "Okay. Let's forget it."

That was the end of it-- I thought.

But it turned out that I wasn't through with Jackie Mason. Later on, before Mason went to Broadway with his one-man show, he needed some break-in dates. This was the late 1980s. For three and a half years I was putting in all the shows at the Sahara Hotel in Las Vegas as an outside promoter. I was getting a lot of big names to come into the hotel strictly on spec with me. Mason was looking for break-in dates, so somehow, someway, I contacted him, and he wound up working for me three times. And I made a lot of money out of his appearances. Of course, Mason made money as well, but he also used these appearances to prepare himself for his Broadway run.

And then Jackie Mason finally told me why he didn't pay me that time we had the "sit-down." It was because of his girlfriend. She used to go to a psychiatrist five days a week and she told Mason stories about me and others that weren't true. She had it all made up that we were out to get him, and he believed her. He bought her stories for quite a while until he finally saw the light and wised up. It was sad to find out what had happened to Mason, but I've got to credit him with opening up to me, leveling with me, and telling me the truth.

Things started to go very badly for me in 1987. I was a big player in the stock market, won and lost almost a quarter of a million dollars on a few occasions. When the crash happened in 1987, I lost a ton of money. At that same time between 1987 and 1991 everything started to go downhill for me. I had Laine Kazan do a TV series that was making $2,000 a week for me in commissions. Suddenly she got fired from the show. I lost that commission. And then everything bad started happening, one thing after another.

Frank Gorshin was crazy. You want an example? We make a two-year deal for him at Harrah's in Atlantic City at $15,000 a week for several weeks each year. Whenever he'd get up on the stage to do his act, he would knock the venue. He kept pointing out things to the audience that was wrong with the place.

The owners would call me: "What is he? Crazy? We're paying him to insult us?"

Not only was Frank Gorshin getting $15,000 a week there, he had gratis suites, food and beverage. Would he keep his mouth shut and enjoy it? No.

I had to fly into Atlantic City. The bosses called me in.

They said, "He's got to stop that. Otherwise, we're going to cancel him."

So I made a speech to Gorshin that night in his room before he went on to do his show.

I said, "Frank, you're going to lose this job.

You've got a golden thing here. Keep your mouth shut."

Frank said, "Okay, okay."

That night Frank Gorshin made his speech again:

"Would you people just look at this place? Just look at these curtains! What're we all doing here-- slumming?"

Harrah's fired Frank Gorshin.

I lost all that commission.

Then another client of mine, Sid Caesar (who I'll tell more about later) fell down while walking his dogs and broke his hip. We had to cancel a bunch of his shows. So I really got hurt financially during this period.

We couldn't afford to live in Beverly Hills anymore. Thank God I still had the Palm Springs house otherwise I don't know where we would have lived. We gave up the Beverly Hills apartment in April 1991.

It was along in this period when my fortunes

began to plummet that I came into conflict with a crazy racket guy who had just come out of Federal Prison by the name of "Johnny Dan." This happened when we still lived in Beverly Hills.

Johnny Dan started to extort money from one of the ex-William Morris agents, a man named Tony Ford. Ford now had a job trying to make television packages for Playboy. Johnny Dan also pressured actor Phil Foster who played "Fazio," LaVerne's father on the TV sitcom *Laverne and Shirley*.

Tony Ford and Phil Foster came to me for advice and help. They knew my family's background and they thought that I could get Johnny Dan to leave them alone. I listened to their stories and realized that they were really the victims of an all-out extortion plot. I told them I would do what I could to help them.

Johnny Dan got wind of Ford and Foster coming to see me, and he started to resent the fact that I was going to become involved. So Johnny Dan and a couple of his henchmen came to our apartment in Beverly Hills. I wouldn't let him in, but I went out into the hall to speak to him.

Johnny Dan always had a threatening way about him, always insinuating that something very drastic was about to happen. He was slight of build with thinning, dark hair. He dressed California casual, slacks and shirt.

In the hall of our apartment, Johnny Dan fidgeted and shifted the weight on his feet as I stood looking at him and his henchmen standing behind him.

"What's with all the muscle?" I asked.

"What's with your nose?" Johnny Dan replied. "Why do you keep stickin' it in places?"

"I'm busy," I said. "What do you want?"

"I want you to butt out," Johnny Dan said.

"Get lost," I said. "All of you. Now."

Johnny Dan shifted the weight on his feet again, and then he turned, nodded to his henchmen and they all left.

Then Johnny Dan went out to Tony Ford's building, positioned himself directly below the executive offices, took aim with a rifle and fired a shot into Tony Ford's window. That was just Johnny Dan's way of getting everybody's attention, to let everybody know that Johnny Dan had big plans in store for us all.

The Playboy people had a security guard parked in front of Tony's house, morning, noon and night.

At that time, I had taken an office in Beverly Hills with George Kane. I was once George's assistant at William Morris. Now he was on his own and he had joined me in my management business.

Johnny Dan waited until George went home for the evening, and then he came walking into the office with one of his henchmen. I was all alone.

Now Johnny Dan really became threatening.

"Hey, Spellman," Johnny Dan said deadpan. Then he flashed a cold grin. Then he went deadpan again.

"What did I tell you?" Johnny Dan asked.

"I don't remember," I said. "Was it

important?"

Johnny Dan sat down on my desk, looming right before me where I sat in my chair.

"Hear about my target practice?" Johnny Dan asked. "I'm getting better since I got out. Next time I can put it right between the eyes."

"What do you want?" I asked.

"What do I want? What do I want?" Johnny Dan repeated. He picked up a letter opener lying on my desk. It was a knife. He fondled it.

"What I want," Johnny Dan said, "is for you to stay out of this-- understand?"

Then Johnny Dan leaned toward me, pointing the letter opener at me, and asked again, "Understand?"

I said nothing.

Johnny Dan came closer to me, swiping the letter opener back and forth, slashing the air with it, repeating, "Understand? Understand? Understand?"

"Just calm down," I said. "Calm down."

I looked right into Johnny Dan's eyes.

Behind the swagger, I could see the fear deep in the back of them. I kept looking at him.

Then I said: "We can work things out."

I kept staring into his eyes. The blade of the letter opener paused in the air.

Suddenly Johnny Dan dropped the letter opener on my desk and stood up. He went to the door and nodded to his henchman. The other guy went out.

Johnny Dan turned to me and said, "You'd better remember what I said this time. Won't be another time."

Then Johnny Dan turned and went out the door.

I knew I had to do something. First, I called my brother-in-law, Ron, and told him what had just happened. Ron, being a lawyer, had to be very official.

Ron said, "Go to the police."

I said, "I can't go to the police! Are you crazy?"

"You asked my advice," Ron said. "That's

the best that I can tell you."

"All right," I said, and hung up.

I knew the police was not the answer, if for no other reason than I had no way of proving what Johnny Dan had said and done in my presence. The police would get involved after there was some evidence, like maybe somebody's dead body turning up, hopefully not mine.

Then I thought of Dino Conte, the guy my father-in-law had introduced me to on the corner of 58th Street and First Avenue in New York. Conte was now in Hollywood. I called him up and told him what had been happening.

"Yeah," Conte said. "I know all about it. That Johnny Dan is crazy. You'd better watch out. Just be sure when you get out of your car to look over your shoulder."

"I can't live that way," I said. "Something has got to be done about that guy."

"You better call your father-in-law," Conte said.

"I hate to bother him," I said.

"You'll have to call him," Conte said. "I can't control Johnny Dan."

So finally I called Joe Straci and told him what had been happening. He told me to come to New York.

I flew to New York. My father-in-law arranged a "sit-down" in East Harlem in a little mob-controlled clubhouse. Johnny Dan's benefactor, a guy named "Dapper Dan," came with his *Consigliere* to make sure that Dapper Dan was getting a fair hearing. On my side was my father-in-law, me and a representative, "Sammy," a student or lieutenant of Buckalo's.

We talked and explained everything. In the whole discourse, it came out that this guy Johnny Dan was wrong in what he had been doing and he was going to have to stop.

So the guys on Johnny Dan's side said, "Okay. We'll put the clamps on him and straighten everything out."

And then my father-in-law said something and I realized why he was so successful in his world. The diplomacy of his thinking came out. It was interesting, because, even though he did it with the "dese, dems and dose" way of speaking, his way of thinking was almost parallel to Nat Kalcheim's who also didn't have a college education, but was a true diplomat and administrator. Both Joe Straci and Nat Kalcheim knew how to handle a "hot" situation.

My father-in-law said, "Hold it. Listen. What he's doing is affecting my family. We have enough heat on us from the law as it is already. As an organization, we don't need any more heat. So *I'll* take the heat. My family will take the heat. We're not going to do anything, rather than draw attention to all of us. As long as Johnny Dan does nothing but talk, we'll listen to him and let him talk until he cools down."

Well, Johnny Dan's people were delighted with what my father-in-law said. And they were very impressed. I saw how these guys backed off and became very cooperative. My father-in-law handled the situation in a very astute way and averted what probably would have turned into a disaster for all of us.

So the Straci family was going to play it out without doing anything to cause a furor.

But then something *did* happen.

I went back to California. I've always said, "There are no secrets."

As soon as I got back, the F.B.I. called me. They wanted me to come in to their office. They told me that they knew all about Johnny Dan. They told me a story about Johnny Dan that was just like the John Gotti story, where his neighbor accidentally killed Gotti's son when the boy ran across the street. Gotti's underling "Sammy the Bull" wanted to kill the neighbor, but Gotti said, "It was an accident." But Gotti's
underlings killed the neighbor anyway. It was the same thing with Johnny Dan. There was a little beef between Johnny Dan's son and the neighbors and Johnny Dan's cohorts took the neighbor and almost killed him. The F.B.I. also knew about how Johnny Dan had been trying to extort Tony Ford.

365

They had been following Johnny Dan. They had been looking for an excuse to put him back in prison. They knew he was a firecracker. They had to get him off the streets before somebody got hurt. They knew that Johnny Dan had come to see me. They knew about the "sit-down" I had just attended in East Harlem.

"You've got to come in," the F.B.I. agent said, "and we want you to tell all about—- "

I said, "Hold it. You're using Johnny Dan as an excuse. Don't tell me it's just about Johnny Dan. You're looking for me to open up about my father-in-law. And you know what's going to happen? You're going to cause turmoil in my personal life. You're going to cause a divorce. Do you really want to cause that?"

The F.B.I. agent was very nice. He said, "Well, there are parts of this job I really don't like myself. So let's put it on hold, and if we have to contact you again, we'll contact you."

I didn't hear from the F.B.I. again, and I was glad. Don't kid yourself. When you get a call from the F.B.I., you start to shiver.

As for Johnny Dan, he backed off. There was just too much heat on him finally from all sides.

In 1979, Cece and I went to Las Vegas on a business trip. While I was booking James Brown into the Sahara, Cece played the slot machines, which she loved to do. She won $5,000 on the slots. She was so excited that she decided to call her mother in New York, even though it was 2 am in New York.

It was the spring of 1983 when Ron Straci called and told Cece that her father had died. Cece was very close to both her parents, but she was very strong, and took the news well. Cece seemed to have a deep understanding of the vicissitudes of life. We flew back to New York for the funeral. Several years later Gigi had to be taken to the hospital. She fell into a coma. Everybody in the family gathered at the Lexington hospital in Manhattan. Gigi was on life support machines.

The doctors recommended pulling the plug. Ron, Sharon and Cece together made the very difficult decision to let their mother go.

In the 1980s I noticed that my sons were starting to grow up. Matthew and Chris have been close throughout their entire lives. But they have each lived their own lives, in their own way. (Sound familiar?)

Matthew and his friends in school were conscious of the soft Rock and Roll like the groups Journey and Bread. This was before the breakthrough of hip-hop and rap and all that real funk music. Matthew was typical of his age. He and all of his friends were all good students and good kids.

In 1984 when Chris was 12, his lifestyle became more radical. He was exemplary of what was going on in his generation, which was only two years nine months difference from his brother Matthew. It was remarkable how Chris and all his friends his age were different from Matthew and his friends. Chris' friends were all from rich families and prominent families: show business, lawyers, business executives, doctors. All of these kids who were friends with Chris were rebels, girls and guys.

We moved to Beverly Hills in 1977. Chris started kindergarten there. Those first years there in Beverly Hills went well for him.

But around 1984, I began to notice changes in Chris and his friends. They started getting into trouble at school, cutting classes, not doing their homework. Then later, when they went to Beverly Hills High School, the girls started with the pink hair, guys with earrings.

CHAPTER FOURTEEN

Laying Down The Law

With Chris, it was always something. When he was about 18 he came home one day with a tattoo on his arm.

Cece was stalwart through all this. She would just say, "That's Chris." She would never get emotional. She was always very, very strong in her composure. Cece was the rock of the family. I was much more emotional.

So Chris was going through this whole experience. But all of the kids Chris' age were going through the same thing. My niece who lived in New Jersey was exhibiting behavior that was like a rubber stamp of what Chris was doing. This continued until on their own Chris and all his peers changed.

It was like a cop once said to me: "Until they straighten themselves out by themselves, they'll go on this way."

Chris was a rebel. It was the James Dean syndrome. The kids of Chris' generation experimented. It was like daring fate. I tried to give Chris as many guidelines as I could. Cece was always the forgiving one.

Chris took an interview with Charles Milne the dean of NYU's film school and was accepted on the spot, even though he hadn't yet taken his S.A.T. A fifteen minute interview lasted an hour and fifteen minutes. Chris and Charles hit it off, smoking cigarettes and chatting about films. Charles said that Chris' list of favorite films was refreshing. Charles also remarked on how Chris' student film was so well edited. Charles was impressed that the film wasn't the usual attempt at the artsy but a Public Service Announcement using Beverly Hills High School student athletes.

Although Chris was accepted into NYU, we got him into San Francisco State which was less expensive. Through mutual friends, we contacted Augusta Coppola, Francis Ford Coppola's brother, who was the dean of their film school. We talked to him about Chris taking courses in film. We got Chris a gorgeous apartment. But then he goofed up and didn't go to class. He lay around smoking. Before six months were up, we brought him back home. Chris' personality was still problematical. From his trip to Russia with his high school senior class to when he attended San Francisco State it was a turbulent coming-of-age period for Chris, a time when he read such books as *Catcher in the Rye* and *On the Road.*

Then we enrolled Chris in community college in Palm Springs where fortunately he got decent enough credits that he could transfer to U.N.L.V. Through my relationship with state Senator Sue Loudon we were able to help facilitate Chris' transfer. Although Chris achieved some high points in his major of English Literature, his grades were erratic. He did, however, learn quite a bit about my business from spending a lot of time with

372

me at the Sahara Hotel. Chris transferred once again, this time to Cal State Northridge. Here, things started to go good, because I think he was enamored with the academia and the level of intellect that prevailed there in the curriculum of English Literature. Northridge was a very good school. Chris was always an insatiable reader. However, he gives credit to his mother, Cece, for helping him graduate with a B.A. in English Literature. Though, I think the fondest memory of that period was when I called a friend and got Chris two tickets to see KISS's first reunion in makeup, and on Halloween of all days.

When Chris graduated from college, he came to me and told me that he was joining the army.

I said, "Are you kidding? That's no place for you."

"No, Dad," Chris said. "I need this. I need the discipline. I have to do this."

Chris joined the army and did well in it. After he got discharged, he came home and we all went to see Al Martino who was headlining at the McCallum Theater in Palm Springs. After the show, we went backstage to the green room.

Al Martino stood up to graciously kiss Cece, but then he saw Chris walk in. Martino had not seen Chris in a long time. Martino knew Chris because Martino's daughter, Allison, had gone to school with Matthew and Chris. When Martino saw how big and muscular Chris had become, Martino said, "A Marine! A Marine!"

The army had really built Chris up physically.

Chris always wanted to be in show business. In a lot of ways, he wanted to be like me, to do the business end of the show. When he was still in high school, I told him that he was going to have to get a college degree and get into a mailroom. So after he graduated from college and did his stint in the army, Chris went out and did arduous interviews at agencies and management companies all over town. Barbara, the HR person at ICM (who Chris will never forget) said that if it were her call, she would have hired him. But after a number of interviews, Chris still wasn't yet hired. Because Cece and I knew Bernie Brillstein, we were able to contact him.

Bernie Brillstein was a major player in the entertainment industry. He had started out in the mailroom at William Morris and became an agent there, just the same way that I did, only he started a few years earlier. He was the WMA agent who serviced Elvis Presley when Elvis made his very first television appearance. In 1960, Bernie discovered a tall, lanky puppeteer who looked like Abraham Lincoln. The guy was Jim Henson, creator of the Muppets. Bernie represented and managed Jim Henson throughout his career, right to the end of Henson's life. Bernie also managed the original players of *Saturday Night Live*, people like John Belushi, Dan Ackroyd and Gilda Radner. Bernie got into creating TV series, such as *Hee-Haw*. He started producing motion pictures. He was a gigantic success. At the time we contacted him, Bernie Brillstein had a major theatrical enterprise that managed Brad Pitt, Jennifer Anniston and other big stars. His company produced *The Sopranos*. They were hot as a pistol.

I knew Bernie from William Morris. I gave Bernie his first client, Norm Crosby when Bernie left WMA to go into the management business with Jerry Weintraub. Before I met Cece, Bernie became acquainted with her at the Englewood Country Club where my father-in-law was a member. A lot of show business people were members there. Bernie had big eyes for Cece and wanted to date Cece in the worst way, but my mother-in-law didn't want Cece marrying a Jewish guy in show business! (Meanwhile, look what happened!) So my mother-in-law got Bernie away from Cece by introducing him to the woman who would become his second wife.

So when Cece called Bernie to talk about Chris getting a shot in his mailroom, Bernie said, "Cece, he's your son. No problem."

Chris went to work for Bernie Brillstein. Just like me, Chris waited an unprecedented fifteen months while others left and few were promoted. At that time Brillstein Grey Entertainment hadn't yet implemented a formal training program and you had to be hired on to a desk. And Chris was. This launched him forward, proudly following in my shoes.

Back in 1983 I was speaking to Bill Knowles, the author of a book about Sid Caesar, entitled *Where Have I Been?* It was a successful book, sold in all the bookstores in Los Angeles. Bill Knowles was recommended to me by the head of the literary department at William Morris when Joey Bishop wanted to do a book called *The Sinatra I Knew*.

Driving back and forth with Bill to Newport Beach for meetings with Bishop, I happened to ask Bill about what was now going on with Sid Caesar, expecting to hear a barrage of events and activities commensurate with the success of the book.

Bill said, "Nothing. He goes to the gym every day."

I said, "What are you talking about?"

Bill said, "Yeah, nothing's going on."

I called Sid Caesar's William Morris agent, Fred Moch, who was the head of the personal appearance department on the West Coast, and asked him, "What's going on with Sid Caesar?"

Moch confirmed what Bill Knowles had told me. Nothing was happening with Sid Caesar.

So I asked Bill Knowles, "Would you introduce me to Sid Caesar?"

So I went with Bill to Sid's house in Beverly Hills, and Bill introduced me to Sid. Sid and I stayed in touch. We talked further, and finally I signed Sid Caesar with my management company. When I say I "signed" Sid Caesar, I never had a written contract with anyone in the personal management business, except Jackie Mason, and he was the only one I ever had trouble with in regard to a client paying me my fee.

I knew I could manage Sid Caesar. I've never been awe struck by stars-- except one.

I was in the Plaza Hotel in New York, going

up the elevator. I turned to my left, looked down and saw...

Lassie!

I flipped, because I've been a dog lover all my life. My first love of a dog was when I was two or three, living in the Bronx. Our neighbor, Mrs. Neusbaum, had a collie, and I used to go upstairs and play with that dog every day.

Lassie was the only star that ever impressed me!

I knew it was Lassie, because they would never have allowed any other dog into the Plaza Hotel. Plus, Lassie's trainer was there, and I asked him, "Is this Lassie?"

And he said, "Yes."

So I was not awe-struck with Sid Caesar, even though he had been touted as a "television legend."

I saw no problem with Sid Caesar at our initial meeting. I represented him for eleven years. The first seven were bliss. He listened to everything I recommended and wanted to do. He

379

would check with me before he would do anything on his own. We had an unbelievable relationship that led to a huge success in the resurgence of his career.

In November 1984, Sid Caesar shook hands with me and we were off and running immediately. I put Sid Caesar in nightclubs. I got lucky and booked Sid for humongous dollars, bigger money than he had ever made at the height of his TV career in the 1950s with *Your Show of Shows*. I got him $40,000 for a two-day weekend in Atlantic City. It was actually a two-weekend booking. He did very, very well and they exercised their option and I got him $50,000 a week. All the other famous comics like Milton Berle and Dick Shawn couldn't believe that I was getting Sid this kind of money. They thought I was lying when I told how much I was getting for Sid. But we were getting every penny of the $50,000. Everything opened up. Success breeds more success. Various talk show hosts and CNN would put together panels with Neil Simon, Mel Brooks, Carl Reiner and Woody Allen, all talking about "the genius of Sid Caesar." Well, they said that loud enough and long enough until the whole country was talking "Sid Caesar."

The fact is: I'm the one who got Sid Caesar's career rolling again. I made it happen. Sid would have never come out of retirement if I hadn't pushed him back into performing.

The producer of *The Hollywood Palace*, Nick Vanoff, once turned to a group of guys he was with, pointed to me, and said, "This is the guy who brought Sid back."

Yes, I brought Sid Caesar back in a big way. I had Sid do lecture tours. I put him in front of symphonies. He did the narrative of *Peter and the Wolf*. He was all over the television map again. He did a whole series of appearances on *Sesame Street*.

Bob Hope was planning his 80th Birthday Special for NBC, and he wanted Sid Caesar on the show to do his gibberish routine about languages. We met at Bob's house to discuss the show. Sitting there in Bob Hope's living room was Bob, Elliott

Kozak, Bob's manager, Sid Caesar and me. We were there to talk about the logistics involved with Sid doing the show.

In mid-twentieth century show business the running gag was that Jack Benny was cheap. But everybody in Hollywood knew that it was really Bob Hope who was the cheapest of all the stars. They said that when Bob Hope pinched a penny, he could make Lincoln cry "ouch." Here was a guy who had made zillions of dollars in show business. He owned land. He owned half of Toluca Lake. But he drove a *Chrysler station wagon*. I'm not saying that he had to have a Rolls Royce, but he drove a *station wagon*.

Bob and the rest of us were talking about flying over to Paris.

Bob said, "Well, we'll fly from LAX to JFK and then we'll have about a five hour wait. Then we'll catch a plane to Paris."

I said, "Bob, what are you doing that for? I mean, you can take LAX, go right over the Artic and you come right down in Paris."

Bob asked me: "Do you know how much money I save going through New York?"

Here, Bob Hope was 80 years old. I don't care what V.I.P. lounge he would sit in at JFK, it would still be five hours, and it would still be *sitting*. And with all his money??? He was going to *save money*??? Why? So he could take it with him??? Talk about cheap and self-denial!

George Schlatter was a famous director and producer of TV specials. On one of Schlatter's specials honoring Sid Caesar with a lifetime achievement award, Sid made a speech and mentioned me. I got up and took a bow on camera. The whole country saw me. The next year, Schlatter did another special. Sid was invited. Carl Reiner was there. Imogene Coca was there. There was no room for me at their table. I was sitting at a table by myself, behind them. At that time, I was bringing shows to the Sahara in Las Vegas.

George Shapiro and Danny Robertson came over to my table and started talking to me. Shapiro was not only Jerry Seinfeld's manager, but he was co-producer of *Seinfeld*. He used to be at William Morris. Danny Robertson was an agent (still is, at the Agency for the Performing Arts). Robertson was a forerunner agent of the "comic explosion." He was the ground floor in finding and developing the hot, new comics. So these two guys, George Shapiro and Danny Robertson come over to my table.

Shapiro and Robertson start pitching me on a new comic. We chatted for a while, and then they walked away.

Then Sandy Wernick, who was a partner with Bernie Brillstein, walks by me. Wernick represented Adam Sandler. Walking behind Sandy was another one of his clients, Jeffery Tambour. Sandy turned and saw me. He and I grew up together as kids in the Bronx.

Sandy Wernick yelled out: "Hey, Jew!"

Okay. We laughed.

I got up and we started talking, but Tambour was trying to hold on to Sandy's attention.

Sandy turned back to Tambour, and said: "Would you wait a minute? I'm talking to a real good friend of mine."

Sandy said that LOUD. So we go on chit-chatting...BLAH, BLAH, BLAH. Then I go back to my table. I sit down at my table. Who sat next to me?

George Schlatter.

I said, "George, it's Larry Spellman."

George remembered me from the year before when we had honored Sid.

George said, "Hey, Larry!"

We talked for a while, and then George said, "The commercial's over. I've got to get back to the set."

So George got up and went away, leaving me alone at my table again after all of these very well-known show business figures had stopped by in succession to speak to me.

Two girls were sitting at the next table. They came over to me.

One of them said, "I'm George Schlatter's

niece. My friend and I have been working on the show. And we've been wondering about something and talking about it and trying to figure it out. And we wondering...can I ask you a question?"

"Sure," I said.

"Who *are* you?"

Yes, fame is fleeting. I had my fifteen seconds on Sid's show and now—- my time was up!

I put Sid on Broadway—- until he started doing what unfortunately happens to these artists. The success goes to their heads. They forget where they came from. In this case, when I started with Sid Caesar, he was totally out of business. So now I get him back in where he is now on top of the world again. It's like Rudyard Kipling's *The Man Would Be King*. It goes to their heads. That's what happened to Sid Caesar.

After seven good years, the next four years were all uphill. Sid didn't do drugs much, but after a performance he would relax with a pipe-full of marijuana. He didn't drink at all.

Around the seventh year of my management, we got an offer for Sid Caesar to do a pilot for a TV series. We do the pilot. Sid wasn't happy with the writing. He wanted to hire another writer and re-vamp it. The pilot was funny. Bud Grant was the head of CBS at that time.

Grant said, "Listen, you guys want to take your time, re-vamp it. We're not going anywhere. Take your time."

But then Bud Grant got fired.

The new administration at CBS said, "We don't want Caesar's show."

We had a commitment from CBS for six shows. They paid us off. We should have been on the air. We should have sold the first pilot as is. It's a lesson. Take what you've got and go with it. It's very fluid in the television and motion picture industries. Today they're here, and tomorrow they're gone, and you never know what it's going to be.

Then Sid Caesar did Broadway.

We started very successfully off-Broadway

at The Village Gate, which was a very special place where people like Bill Cosby played. Arthur D'Lugoff was a fine impresario who had a great talent and knew how to promote it. We did *Sid Caesar and Company*. A lot of celebrities came there to see Sid: Lauren Bacall, Rod Steiger, Cy Coleman. Word got out how hot we were. Ira Blacker had a big hit on Broadway as the producer of *Ma Rainey's Black Bottom*. Blacker came in and took Sid to Broadway.

This shows how flaky show business is, how you're considered "only as good as your last time out." Sid Caesar had all these years of success in television, in lectures, in symphonies. Famous celebrities were falling all over themselves on national television proclaiming Sid Caesar the greatest genius since Einstein and Leonardo Da Vinci. Did it mean anything? Did it count for anything?

Not when it came time to get Sid ready to go to Broadway, it didn't. The fiasco happened this way:

Sid was performing at the Village Gate. We were doing great there for three months, packing them in.

D'Lugoff said, "Stay here and keep the show up, because after Labor Day the Jews will come back from the Catskills. Then we'll really pack 'em in!"

But Sid got antsy, antsy, like it was so important and urgent for him to go back home.

Ira Blacker wanted to have a very hot Broadway director, Jerry Zacks, direct the show. But Zacks was in Europe.

Ira said, "Stay here at the Village Gate another month. Jerry Zacks will come back."

Sid said, "No, no, no."

So instead of staying at the Village Gate, we compromised and took what I thought was a lesser director, even though this guy was hot with the big hit *Annie*. This director starts in to "fix" Sid's show. Here's another lesson to live by on Broadway: "If it's not broke, don't fix it!" Sid's show didn't need fixing. It wasn't broke. It was the exact opposite. It was hot. It was packing the house every night. It was grabbing the audience in their seats, sending everybody into gales of laughter. The show was a *brilliantly polished diamond*! The biggest stars were fans of the show! Ira Blacker was flipping over Sid's show! This success of Sid's show was the whole reason why we were going to Broadway with it in the first place! And then, my main point: here was Sid, the "television legend," the great "genius of comedy," and now we had to get outside advice from a "director" on how to "really make the show ready for Broadway"?

Give us all a break.

They brought in "what's-his-name" to direct. He changed so many things around that he literally ruined the show. People asked me, "Why didn't Sid do it the way he did it at the Village Gate?" My answer was: the director wouldn't let him, and I couldn't stop the director. And that's why Sid Caesar's show died on Broadway.

One time Sid Caesar and I were sitting,

having a meeting with Martin Charnin who started his career writing acts for performers. Then he got hot with a director.

I said, "Hey, Marty-- "

He said, "It's Martin."

That's the pretense with the theatre crowd. I call it the "Sardi's Syndrome" after the famous restaurant in the heart of the New York Theatre District. These "thee-ah-tuh" people get so affected. They have blinders on.

I was having a meeting with a group of producers at Sardi's and we were talking about *A Chorus Line*. What a put-down I got when I told them that I had only seen the show once.

"You mean you've only seen it *once*?" they sneered.

Well, I thought the show was good, but I didn't flip over it. But they're attitude was like: "No! How could you?" The died-in-the wool "thee-ah-tuh" people really have blinders on. They're in their own world.

After the Broadway flop, *Sid couldn't get a*

job. I couldn't get a job for him. We were, like, out of business! As I said, "You're only as good as your last time out." Everybody completely forgot everything that Sid had done for the eight years prior to his Broadway flop.

So now it's over, right? I got discouraged. It *did* get to me. I was really taken aback by the negative response. It was Sid who pumped *me* up.

He said, "C'mon. Let's get another project going. We'll just get something going. It'll inspire us. We'll get going."

That's when a light bulb went off in my head about seeing if I could get Imogene Coca to come back to work.

When I asked her, Imogene said, "Yes."

She was already about 80 years old.

So I put Sid Caesar and Imogene Coca together again and I called it just that: *Sid Caesar and Imogene Coca Together Again*.
We opened at a nightclub on the east side of Manhattan called Michael's Pub. We stayed open

there for eleven straight weeks. Michael's Pub was where Mel Torme would play and where Woody Allen and his band would play on some nights. We re-kindled the whole thing with Sid and Imogene and we had successful tours all over the country after that.

I produced two Friars Roasts at the Sahara in 1992. The first was for Sid Caesar. On the dais were Milton Berle, Henny Youngman, Foster Brooks, Jackie Gayle and Slappy White. Gayle was a real nightclub comic. Slappy White was an exponent of the real Harlem/New York humor. Gayle was the crème-de-la-crème on the Playboy Circuit. About six months later, we did a second roast. We roasted Zsa Zsa Gabor. On the dais for the second roast was Sid Caesar, Jackie Gayle, Shelley Berman, Slappy White and Freddie Roman as the MC. Roman was also the Dean of the Friars.

The first roast was really iconic of the Friars. Milton Berle, Sid Caesar and Henny Youngman were on the stage together. They were very funny. And they drew a big crowd. The 800 seats were packed. Jerry Lewis, who reputedly never came to see anybody else's show in Vegas, came to see this show. In the three and a half year history of all the shows I brought to the Sahara, the bosses never came to any of the shows. The entertainment director never came to any of the shows. But that show with Milton, Sid and Henny, the bosses came to that, both the entertainment director and the owner, Paul Loudon. Polls said that his wife, Sue Loudon, could beat Harry Reed for the U.S. Senate in Nevada. She came out with that stupid line about using a chicken to barter with your doctor. It ruined everything and she lost out.

The Friars Club had a great steam room and gym. It was where all the celebrities could let their hair down and be themselves. The Friars also had guys on the periphery of show business, but they were charismatic, like a famous tobacconist by the name of Nat Sherman. You also had garment center guys in the Friars. There was a professional category and a non-professional category in the club. The non-professionals paid a lot more money to join, but they all wanted to be there. The Friars, at any one time, had as many as 1,000 members. It was big. They were famous for putting on Roasts way before the Dean Martin Roasts.

Originally the Friars Roasts were for men only. The ballrooms of the different hotels that they would rent would sell out immediately. Every four-letter word went. That was what they were famous for. The Friars in New York held luncheons. The West Coast Friars would hold their events in the evening. Johnny Carson would MC one year. You would never know who was going to be there. Years later I think Phyllis Diller dressed up like a man so that she could get in. Then there was a movement on to allow women into the Roasts. Women performers were almost ready to sue the Friars Club for being exclusively male. The club was going to lose its non-profit status. So they had to let the women in. All the men thought that the women were going to be squeamish about all their raw humor. The joke was on the men. The guys on the dais *did* say the four-letter words, but you know who laughed the loudest? The women.

After Imogene Coca left our production, Sid Caesar's career went down again. Sid started to smoke marijuana a lot more. He was becoming difficult to be with. He started fighting me in bad ways on things that were totally wrong. He was making bad decisions. It was causing tremendous negative reactions among the guys in show business. I bit my tongue during this time, because I needed Sid for that second Friars Roast I was producing. But I knew that once that was over with, I was going to terminate my business relationship with Sid.

The conflict between Sid Caesar and me came to a head when I booked him into the Fontainebleau Hotel in Miami. It was the height of the season and the hotel was booked to capacity. But Sid insisted that he had to have a room with a balcony. (He wanted the balcony so that he could smoke his marijuana pipe.) I talked to the guy who ran the Fontainebleau and told him that Sid was insisting on a room with a balcony or he wouldn't do his show.

The guy said, "Are you sure? Can I talk to him?"

I said, "Be my guest. Here's his number."

I gave him Sid's number.

In a few minutes, the guy called me back, and said, "Let's forget the whole deal."

That's how Sid Caesar turned people off, and I knew I had to end it with him, right then and there.

My relationship with Cece was always fine, except for the arguments we had over Chris when he was growing up. Cece wanted to baby him. I wanted to toughen him. Somehow, between us, everything worked out all right with Chris. Or maybe I should say, in fairness, Chris worked things out all right for himself in the end. I began to see that Chris was really *me, all over again*. He was a law unto himself. He just had to find his own way, as we all do.

Cece worked with me hand-in-hand. She did my secretarial work, my filing, all the detail stuff. She was great at it. And, of course, she was a great diplomat for me. Cece used to "wow" everybody. She made friends wherever she went. Me, I was strictly business, straight-ahead and matter-of-fact.

Cece was a great hostess at parties. She was "the woman behind the man." I don't know what I would have done without her. She made my life. She *was* my life. We worked together, side-by-side. We played together, side-by-side. We were together all the time, all the way, in everything.

In the late 1980s and early 1990s I was very successful in bringing shows to the Sahara in Las Vegas. All these guys trusted me and what I could do. Each of these shows I produced ran about ten days, Friday to the following Sunday. Then we would take off Monday, Tuesday and Wednesday. Then we would start another cycle.

So I had Jackie Mason, Neil Sedaka and

Steve Allen with *The Original Tonight Show*. Allen's show was just like his original TV show in the 1950s with Bill Dana, Louie Nye, Marilyn May and the Bill Smith Trio. I booked into the Sahara Cool and the Gang, Little Richard and James Brown.

Here is an interesting study about selling and marketing:

I raised the ticket prices drastically on James Brown. The casino boss and the entertainment director were on my neck about it.

I said, "I know that the people are going to come. James Brown has tremendous fans and he's very hot with them. They'll be glad to pay the higher prices."

Sure enough, James Brown did big business. His audiences gladly paid that extra tab. The bosses were thrilled with the box office, and their confidence in my strategies increased. The lesson was that if you got what people really want, they will pay premium prices to get it, especially in entertainment.

But here is a lesson related to that one, sort of its opposite corollary: I found that if you had an attraction nobody wanted to see, you couldn't even give it away. Even if you would comp people, they wouldn't come.

I had that with Suzanne Somers. Sweet girl, but I couldn't do any business with her. The audience wouldn't come.

Then, you want to talk about ego?

Cybil Shepard.

This was just after her TV series *Moonlighting*. She believed in her own press. God only knows who she thought she was.

I booked her during the Thanksgiving weekend where if I could have headlined Billy Carter (remember that President's brother?) I would have still done brisk business. It all looked like a sure thing.

Cybil Shepard comes in for those four days and she wanted to replicate what Streisand had done when she played Las Vegas. She didn't say "Barbara Streisand" on the marquee, she just had:

"BARBARA". Sinatra, when he played Caesar's Palace, just had on the marquee: "FRANK". So Cybil Shepard insisted that her marquee read: "CYBIL".

I said, "Who's going to know what that means?"

Oh, no. She had to be like...*the real stars*!

And sure enough, she didn't even play the four days that we had booked her. She pulled out the fourth day. She took a bath. She didn't draw anybody, just because of stupid ego. And everybody, her agent, her press agent, everybody was walking on eggs with her.

The last thing I brought to the Sahara was a show called *Bee Hive* which was a sell-out at the Village Gate. It was a revue with five or six girls and a five-piece band. *Bee Hive* referred to the hair-do that the girls wore in the 1960s. It was a revue of girls recreating singing groups in the sixties, and it was a big hit. It was nice to go out on top.

Although my time as a Las Vegas producer drew to a close, I was by no means finished in show business. Just around the corner, one of the most exciting projects of my career lay ahead, a one-man Broadway show starring Frank Gorshin!

CHAPTER FIFTEEN

Say Good Night, Gracie

Frank Gorshin and I got very friendly when I was a young agent at William Morris. Those above me were already starting to respect my opinions. Gorshin made a name for himself on the West Coast and the agents asked us to book him, which we did, at a famous summer resort in the Poconos called Tamiment. The office sent me up there to review Gorshin for a report.

Well, Gorshin was mind-boggling. When he did an impression of Kirk Douglas, he *became* Kirk Douglas. When he did an impression of anybody, he *was* that person. He looked like the person. He felt like the person. His talent was real, but so was his craft. He worked hard at his act, until the effort didn't show, only the magic.

I talked to Frank after his show, and told

him how good I thought he was. Then Frank and I hung out together at the pool. A lot of girls were around. This was when I was single, in the early sixties. Frank and I really hit it off. We were having a blast, telling jokes, making the girls giggle and laugh. I was telling jokes. Frank was telling jokes. We had a crowd around us.

We stayed friendly. I booked Frank Gorshin into the Latin Quarter based on my review of what I had seen him do in the Poconos, plus I gave an unbelievable report to the rest of the office. So I helped launch his career that way.

Then Frank Gorshin started getting really hot. He landed the role of the Riddler on the TV series *Batman*. He was on the show's premiere episode, a two-parter, and he really went over the top in his role. America was watching. The show became a fad, a craze. It was exciting to kids and hilarious for adults. Everybody watched it, and they all loved Frank as the Riddler. Frank became a semi-regular on the series and even made a spin-off *Batman* movie. His career went white-hot.

Demand for his personal appearances soared around the country. He was hot on television, too. Other shows wanted him for a guest star. He rode the wave of all this.

Then later on Frank and I got together again because Joe Scandore and I signed him in the management business. When I left Scandore, Gorshin came with me. Frank was with me for thirteen years.

While we were still with Scandore, we booked Frank Gorshin to open for the Jackson Five. This is just a typical example of the craziness and self-destructiveness of many of these performers. Frank Gorshin was so talented that he could have been an international giant in theatre and entertainment, if he just had not been so "nuts."

I went to Las Vegas to "service" the engagement, as we call it. That is, I was there to see to the needs of our client in regard to whatever might come up foreseen or unforeseen. In this case our client was Frank Gorshin.

They're serving dinner there at the MGM

showroom. So while the waiters are cleaning up the last of the knives, forks and dishes, they're making an announcement: *"Ladies and gentlemen, the MGM is proud to present the Jackson Five with guest star Frank Gorshin."*

After opening night, Frank called me the next morning, and said, "I don't want the recorded announcement to say 'with Frank Gorshin.' I want it to say '*and* Frank Gorshin.'"

I said, "Frank, who's even listening to the tape anyway? The knives and forks are going making noise and that announcement is a two second thing. Nobody's even hearing it."

Frank said, "I don't care. I want them to change it."

Frank Gorshin refused to go on and do his show until the recorded announcement was changed to "and."

Bernie Rothkopf was the entertainment director. He was the nephew of a guy who was partners with Moe Daelitz. They were the Jewish mob from Cleveland and they were the big money behind the MGM. This was before Kirk Kerkorian got in there.

Bernie Rothkopf said, "If it wasn't for you and your family, I'd throw this bum out in two seconds. It's going to cost me union fees to re-record."

Again, here's where my relationship with the mob made it possible to take care of things for my clients. They *did* re-record the announcement. Gorshin felt that the word "with" made him subservient to the Jackson Five. But he was making $30,000 a week. That was Frank Gorshin's whole syndrome. He did things like that all along.

Brilliant as Frank Gorshin was, and he *was* brilliant, he was on a perennial self-destruct course. Everyone in the business knew that Gorshin was brilliant. Other impressionists studied Gorshin's act like it was a master's class. Rich Little, as great an impressionist as he was, used to come in and see Gorshin's show and come back stage and talk to him.

Frank, though, was always on self-destruct.

In Atlantic City, I sent a major agent out to see Frank with a view towards setting up a tour. Frank was brilliant when the agent saw him. The agent was supposed to meet Frank after the show. Frank *knew* that the agent had come out all the way from New York just to see him. But Frank disappeared!

I said to him later: "What the heck is wrong with you? Why weren't you backstage in your dressing room?"

Frank said, "That bass player! Did you hear the bass player in my show? He screwed it all up!"

I said, "That's all you care about? I brought Klaus Kolmar out to see you!"

Frank did things like that all throughout his career.

When I booked Frank Gorshin in Reno, he wouldn't come to the press party that the hotel had thrown for him. He was just off the wall. This was why nobody wanted to handle Frank Gorshin.

Then the time came when we were living full-time in Palm Springs. I was still managing Frank Gorshin. I was in L.A. on some business.

Gorshin was doing an independent film which was a take-off on the hit movie *Oh, God!* Frank was doing the George Burns part, you know, "God." (Don't ask me how they could do a take-off on something that was already a send-up farce to begin with.)

I, being the manager, knew that I had to be on the set of this movie in which Frank Gorshin was co-starring. I figured that I would be perfunctory, spend forty-five minutes on the set, and then take off and head down for Palm Springs.

I sat there and watched them film this thing. It was just terrible. They never finished making it. All I could think as I watched this excrement was: *Oh, God!* The guy who financed the film also wrote it, directed it, and starred in it. Talk about making yourself look bad! He could do it to himself three different ways. And talk about ego! I was ready to get up and leave after the first five minutes, but something strange happened. Rather than just showing my face on this set, I wound up staying there for six hours!

You see, I was in awe of what Frank Gorshin was doing. He was light-years beyond the rest of the cast and the script they were shoveling at him. Frank wasn't just doing an impression of George Burns, *he was doing a reincarnation.*

I said to him, "Frank, you know, this is a one-man show for Broadway."

Frank said, "What is?"

I said, "You as George Burns. It's a great one-man show. I can see it!"

Frank said, "No."

I said, "Yes! Think about it. Stop and think about it."

Frank thought a minute, and then he said, "You know, maybe you've got an idea there."

And that's how the hit Broadway show *Say Good Night, Gracie* started, with me conceiving the show right there on the set of that little, low-budget movie. But it took five years for us to get it off the ground. I had no idea that it would take five years, right then.

And I had no idea that before those five

years was up my life would be shattered into a thousand pieces.

CHAPTER SIXTEEN

Who Promises Tomorrow?

I wanted to get my idea of the one-man George Burns play with Frank Gorshin on to Broadway, but it was initially met with indifference whenever I brought it up. I knew I would have to find and build the right team with myself as a Broadway producer to make my idea happen.

I talked to a friend of mine who was an agent, Chris McNeil, and explained my concept. He put me in touch with his friend, Bill Franzlau, who had toured the show *Beatlemania*. Franzlau was currently having success producing a one-man show called *A Male Intellect/An Oxymoron*. It was appearing on La Cienaga in L.A., so I went to see it, and it was terrific. I met with Bill, and we talked. He agreed to take the reins and help me produce my idea.

We needed someone to write the script for Frank's show. It couldn't just be a stand-up comedy monologue. We needed a real one-man play with a dramatic arc. This is an absolute must in order to hold an audience in a theatre for two hours. We found Rupert Holmes to write the script. Holmes was a very versatile, prolific guy. He was a writer. He was a recording artist. He had a hit record called *Pina Coloda*. He both wrote the song and recorded it. He was an author of books. He made history in the theatre. He won three Tonys for the same property: *The Mystery of Edwin Drood*. He wrote the book, music and lyrics for the show. We believed that Rupert Holmes was the right guy for our project.

Gorshin was appearing at Atlantic City at the Claridge Hotel. I took Rupert and his assistant with me to the Claridge, and they saw Frank's show and flipped.

Rupert got really excited about writing the one-man play. He read four biographies about George Burns and then met with Ron Burns who was George Burns' adopted son. With all that research, Rupert wrote such a brilliant full-length script that we didn't know what to cut. It was so long it had to be cut, but it was all such gold, we just didn't know what to leave out. We titled Frank's one-man show *Say Good Night, Gracie* after George Burns' famous tag line to his wife, Gracie Allen.

I tracked down George Burns' accountant, Bernie Landau. I found out that he was the guy to speak to about getting the rights to George Burns' life story. George Burns had already passed away.

Bernie the accountant said, "Ron Burns is coming over to my house in Encino. Come on over."

I was in Palm Springs on Labor Day weekend and didn't want to go all the way over there.

Bernie said, "Do you want this deal or not?"

I said, "Okay, I'll be there."

When I got over to the accountant's house in Encino, it only took three minutes for me to make the deal with Ron Burns. But we stayed three hours. You want to know why?

Bernie and I started talking about games that kids played in New York when we were growing up in the Bronx there, games that Ron Burns, who had grown up in California, had never heard of: stick ball, stoop ball, ring-a-levio, hop-scotch, and then-- the big game that Ron was really interested in-- Johnny on the Pony. It took three hours of talking back and forth because Ron wanted a detailed explanation of all these games.

You see, we didn't have money in those days. We were kids, nobody had money. We made up our own fun. It was all street games.

In Johnny on the Pony you had two teams. One team would form a "pony" by bending down; you'd put your head underneath the legs of the guy in front of you; the guy behind you did the same thing. One teammate acted as the "pillow," so that a guy's legs rested against the "pillow." Members from the second team would jump on to the first team's backs, and once the whole of the second team jumped on to the back of the "pony," the "pillow" would yell out: "Johnny on the Pony-- one—- two—- three! Johnny on the Pony-- one-- two-- three! Johnny on the Pony-- one-—two—- three!" If the "pony" didn't break, then the second team had to be the pony and the first team would jump on them. These are the kind of games we all made up because nobody had any money. Bernie and I took three hours to tell Ron Burns what these things were all about, and he ate up every one of our words.

All these technological toys today for kids cost hundreds of dollars and we're all buying our kids cars. At 17, Matthew was a good kid and I bought him a brand-new car. But in my childhood, nobody did that. We were poor. In those days, you were glad to just be able to go home and have food on the table. So when it came to having fun, we just made up our own games. Really, I was lucky, because it sparked creativity in me that I used later when I became an agent and producer.

On May 2nd, 2000, Cece and I celebrated our 32nd wedding anniversary. I gave Cece a drop-dead gorgeous ring, very expensive.

Cece said, "This is the kind of gift you give at twenty- five years or fifty years."

I said, "You know, Cece, I was thirty-two when I married you. We've been married thirty-two years, so it's like a lifetime to me. And, after all, Cece, who's promising us tomorrow?"

The next month Cece saw a discoloration on her breast and went to the doctor. They started doing tests.

It was cancer.

Cece took the news calmly. She was very strong and at peace with whatever life held in store for her. I was not so strong.

The doctors decided not to do surgery, only chemotherapy. This treatment lasted six months. Chemo is rough. You lose your hair. You get very tired. It's not easy. The chemo is actually a poison in the body, trying to kill the cancer. The chemo seemed to be working, and Cece was in remission.

In January 2001, the doctors said, "Let's get more aggressive with a new chemo."

One morning I woke up and saw that Cece was gasping for breath; she couldn't breathe. I should have called 911, but I figured it was related to the cancer, so I got her in the car and took her to Desert Hospital in Palm Springs to see her oncologist.

In the hospital, the staff immediately put an oxygen mask on Cece. And then-- the irony—- talk about inefficiency in hospitals!

I'm in the cancer section of the hospital.

The doctor said to me: "I have to have some other doctors look at her. This is not cancer. She can't breathe. So I'm going to get her over to the emergency ward."

The doctor takes out his cell phone, and—- can you believe this-- *calls 911*?! The doctor calls 911 to come take Cece to the emergency ward *in the very same hospital*!

The doctor said to me: "Believe it or not, you can get her into emergency quicker with the paramedics coming to take her in."

We had to wait for outside paramedics to come into the hospital to take Cece to the emergency ward. Here was a doctor trying to get doctors *in the same hospital* to look at Cece. I couldn't believe it!

The paramedics came and took Cece away. The hospital put her in intensive care. I thought about the breathing problem Cece had on our honeymoon, and wondered if her present breathing difficulties were related to it, if maybe the chemo aggravated some kind of hidden lung condition. The doctors never found out.

Cece was in the hospital for three months.

At two in the morning of Monday, April 23rd, 2001, the ringing of the phone awakened me.

I knew Cece was gone.

I got up and answered the phone.

A nurse's voice told me: "Your wife has just passed away." I was numb with shock.

I asked, "Are you going to hold her there so I can say goodbye to her?"

The nurse said, "Yes, but we can't hold her too long."

I rushed over to the hospital, and went into the room.

Cece was there, finally free from all pain. I sat down next to her. I took off Cece's marriage ring, and held her in my arms. I kissed her and talked to her. I sat there with her, all alone for forty-five minutes. Then the nurses came, and said I had to go. I went out into the corridor. I knew I had to call people. I knew I had to keep myself going, had to keep myself living.

I called Chris who was living in L.A. in a studio apartment. It was the hardest phone call I ever made in my life. I told him the news. There was no way to soften it. We had seen it coming, but there was just no preparing. Our conversation was short and brutal for us both. We managed to say goodbye to each other quietly. I next called Cece's brother, Ron Straci. It was five in the morning in New York. Ron's wife, Sharon, answered. Ron wanted to get hold of Matthew before he left for the office.　Matthew lived in an apartment in Ron's townhouse, and he usually left for work around five. Sharon was able to grab Matthew as he was on his way out.

The next day, Ron, Sharon and Matthew flew out and Chris drove down.

Cece had wanted to be cremated.　We had the service on Friday.　The place was packed. Everybody we knew showed up.　All of Cece's friends from Palm Springs and L.A. came.　Guys I knew from the William Morris office came.

Ron and everybody left the next day.　The roughest thing was going back a couple of days later to get the urn that contained Cece's ashes. When I got the urn, I realized that I could not bring myself to dispose of it.　I put the urn on the night table in our bedroom on Cece's side of the bed.　I kept the urn there for years.

I couldn't bring myself to discard Cece's clothes.　I kept all her clothes, all her personal possessions.

I could not accept that Cece was gone.　She

was such a wonderful woman, wife and mother. We did everything together. We were together all of the time. Everything I did, everything I planned, always was arranged according to the needs and desires of Cece. Even the smallest things I did, I now realized, had been given a kind of meaning because they somehow, in some way, related to Cece. Wherever I went when I worked, if I left Cece behind, I always knew that Cece was home, and that I would be coming home to her.

But now Cece was not home. The house was empty. She was not there and she was not coming back, ever, in all eternity. I could not force that impossible idea into my mind and heart. I was lost. I no longer had a sense of direction.

I could not work. I would sit at home, looking about the empty house that once had been brimming over with happiness. Now it was empty of meaning. I tried to reach back into the past with my memories, but it was agonizing. My Frank Gorshin project *Say Good Night, Gracie* was still in development, but I could no longer work on it.

Thank God Bill Franzblau kept the project going at this time. If it hadn't been for Bill, I don't know if *Say Good Night, Gracie* would have ever made it to the stage.

Some days were better than others. I would think that I was getting a handle on my emotions, and then some little thing would happen to me to trigger my grief, and I would collapse in tears. I did my grieving in private as best I could, but everyone around me knew that I was not myself.

During the first days after Cece's passing I got calls from guys around the country that I hadn't spoken to in twenty years. They called to tell me how sorry they were when they heard about Cece. I was very elated by these calls, and felt like I had done something right in my life. I realized that my biggest accomplishment was the marriage that Cece and I had. I had been a very rich man. And also I felt with these calls that people thought enough of me, all the things and relationships I had with them through the years, to take the time and effort to call me. I thought that somewhere along the way I had done something right with all these people, something good. My life had been a success—- not just a money success—- but a people success, where, in the end, I realized, it really counts.

The emotional support of all my family and friends really helped me, but it wasn't enough to heal me. Many times I would cry in pain.

Sometimes guys would call and try to pump me up: "Come on. You're a tough guy. You're a strong guy. You're formidable. Intrepid. You can't fall apart like this."

Sometimes the pain in my body would become so intense, I couldn't stand it. I would be sitting in the house, and my hands would start hurting. I would go into the bathroom and run hot water on my hands, trying to burn away the pain. The thought of suicide crossed my mind, but I pushed the idea away.

It got where I couldn't stand to be in the silent, empty house all alone. I would get in the car and start driving with no planned destination. I would just keep going, following the nothingness of the road ahead. I would get out into the desert somewhere and turn around. I'd drive back to Palm Springs, back to the house, back to its rooms that were still silent and empty.

One day I just drove for a long time. I got into L.A. traffic, turned off the freeway, and drove along the surface streets heading west. I finally reached the Santa Monica pier, stopped the car, got out, and looked around. The sky was gray overhead, and rain started coming down. The pier was wet and deserted. The ocean was breaking wildly on the beach.

I got back in my car, and kept driving. I followed the highway around the beach. Somewhere around Malibu I turned my car up into the hills. The rain was now pouring down in sheets.

I drove higher and higher along the curving road, the rain pouring down. I switched my windshield wipers to top speed. I thought of turning around, but could see no place to do it. The road was narrow. I kept going. I passed a sign that said "Rock Slide Area."

I now found myself driving along a narrow road cut against a mountainside. The other side of the road dropped off almost vertically into a canyon. Water was pouring down in sheets along the sheer, muddy wall of the mountain. I could see small pebbles actually sliding down in the wash.

I pulled my car to a stop against the sheer wall of the mountain, and cut the engine. The rain was pelting the rooftop hard. I could see ahead a slope in the wall of mud, a grassy slope leading to a small hill. I decided that I would get out of the car, run up the hill, and take a look at the road up ahead to see what I was in for. If the road conditions up ahead looked worse, I would try to turn around where I was at, although the road was narrow and the drop was deep on the other side.

I got out of the car and ran toward the grassy slope, got to it, and started my climb. The ground at my feet was much softer than I had expected, and soon my shoes were sinking in quicksand-like mud. I changed the direction of my climb, circling around the little hill as I climbed upward. I came upon

426

some small scrub bushes, grabbed hold of them and used them to propel me forward. I had worked my way almost around to the other side of the hill when I looked down and saw that the ground at my feet was drastically changing its angle. I looked further down and saw that the other side of this little hill dropped off something like one hundred feet to solid ground below. I had climbed my way to the edge of a precipice. My feet started sliding in the mud. I could feel myself going down.

For an instant I thought: go ahead, fall.

But in the next instant, by a deep survival reflex, my hand shot out and grabbed hold to one of the scrub bushes. I started pulling myself up, but my feet were going out from under me. Then the mud below shifted, and I went down in the mud, still grasping the bush, although I could feel its roots start to give way in the earth. The rain was coming down in torrents, covering me in mud.

I shouted out: "Cece! Cece! Let me die here! Let me die!"

I could let go of the bush and it would all be

over.

But then I thought of my two sons, Matthew and Chris. I could see their faces. I knew I had to live. I had to live for them.

I shouted: "Matthew! Chris! Let me live! Let me live!"

I pulled hard on the bush. I got my footing. I pushed up. I climbed. I kept climbing, kept moving up through the rain.
I took a final step.

I stood on top of the hill, covered in mud.

From where I stood, I could see all of the hills and canyon around me. Lightning struck along the distant skyline. I turned to the north and saw that the road ahead was clear.

"Let me live," I said, "Oh God, let me live."

I never believed in therapy and all that. I thought all that stuff was hog wash. Guys used that as a crutch to explain why they were weak. That's what I said-- until it happened to me.

At the hospital, the social worker

recommended a therapy group that was there. So I went to it. The lady who did the counseling for this group was an ex-nun. I did four or five sessions with them. What I found in the group was that other people who lose loved ones experience exactly the same thing I had. I was not unique. I found that my reaction was a natural phase in the cycle of human life. I started reading books about grief management. I learned the common denominators of grief. The opening line of one of the books read, "You are probably going to contemplate suicide. Here is why you shouldn't." The thought of suicide is obviously a thing that permeates all people who go through the experience of profound grief. After reading the books, I started seeing a personal therapist. I went half a dozen times.

The period of extreme, shocked grief lasted a full year and a half for me. I hadn't been going out of the house or seeing anybody. The end of it came when my friends all started doing something very effective. *They started yelling at me.*

They all said, "You can't go on like this! You've got to start living again, meeting people. Going on dates. You don't have to fall in love again. You don't have to get romantic. Take a girl for coffee. Get a conversation going."

My friend Lenny Green fixed me up. Before he came to California, Lenny owned one of the hot nightclubs called Basin Street East. He fixed me up with a nurse he had met in the hospital. It took me two years before I was able to go out on my first date with the nurse.

What helped also was that Frank Gorshin had finally made it to Broadway with *Say Good Night, Gracie*. First, I went to Ft. Lauderdale, Florida for the show's break-in. Then I went to New York for the Broadway opening. I was surrounded by family. Chris and Matthew were there. *Say Good Night, Gracie* was a big success. Gorshin set the audience on fire. The show was Gorshin's greatest hurrah. He was a triumph in the role. The role of George Burns was much bigger for Frank Gorshin than the Riddler on *Batman* ever was. I'm glad I gave him the opportunity to show the world what a fine actor he was before he passed away. And I'm grateful to Frank Gorshin and Bill Franzblau. The show helped me get back into the groove of life.

But, of course, wouldn't you know? Gorshin always had to be Gorshin. On opening night of *Say Good Night, Gracie* Frank didn't want to go to the party afterwards. That was him. I tried to coax him. His wife yelled at him.

I said to Frank: "You've got to go. Are you crazy? All these people are showing up for you! Are you out of your mind? This is your show!"

It was his show, a one-man show, and it was *his* party-- and he didn't want to go to it! He was just ornery. It got to a point where it hurt his career.

Of course, Gorshin was absolutely thrilled by the accolades from the press. He was brilliant. The biggest stars came to see him. They would come backstage and see him every show. We had a great eleven-month run on Broadway. The show was nominated for a Tony Award.

We were looking to put the National Company together for *Say Good Night, Gracie*. Gorshin was going to go on tour, and he wanted Rich Little to finish out the last couple of months on Broadway. Rich auditioned, but he couldn't cut the mustard. He was dying to do it.

What happened: I was at the Beverly Hills Friars Club, having lunch. Rich and his manager were at the next table. They came over to talk to me about *Say Goodnight, Gracie*, and right in front of everybody in the dining room Rich Little got up and started doing his impression of George Burns, to show me that he could do it.

I said, "I knew you could do the impression. But this is an *acting* job. There's a script and all that."

Rich said, "I want to try it."

Rich Little flew to New York to audition for the director and the co-producer. He didn't cut it. They all worshipped, they all looked up to Frank Gorshin, and they were looking for a performer on his level. The difference between Rich Little and

Frank Gorshin was that Frank was an *actor*. Frank not only changed his voice to accommodate the impression, he literally changed his face. When he did Burt Lancaster or Jack Nicolson, you were actually looking at those guys. It was scary! And then Frank could take that intense illusion and tell a story with it, bring the character through a dramatic experience. Rich Little could just do the voice impression as a bit, and it was all on one level, just part of a nightclub act. So we had to turn Rich down.

It took a lot of coaxing to get Gorshin to go on the road with the show. He broke everybody's chops. It was a hard time. There was a lot of yelling to force him to do things. Eventually we just couldn't take Frank Gorshin anymore and couldn't use him anymore. We started looking around for another actor to do *Say Good Night, Gracie*.

I replaced Frank Gorshin with Jamie Farr who had been Klinger on *M*A*S*H*. We met in Palm Springs for lunch with his agent.

Jamie asked, "You think I could be George Burns?"

I said, "You know something, Jamie? I can't do what you do on stage, but I've got my own talent, which is: I have a *vision*. I can see things. And I tell you: You're going to kill playing George Burns. When you perform this, they're going to believe you are George Burns."

Rich Little couldn't do George Burns as a character in a stage play, even though he was a great impressionist, but Jamie Farr could play George Burns because he was an *actor*.

Jamie took the show on the road, but he was already hitting 80 and the road was a little too much for him. He couldn't do an extensive tour.

I did continue with Frank Gorshin, booking him in different places. But he smoked three packs of cigarettes a day, and he eventually contracted throat cancer. He died at about the age of 71. He was a great talent.

Accepting my wife's death was very

difficult. It didn't happen for me all at once. There was no magic solution. It happened in stages, and I worked through each and every one of them. You don't name the stages, you just feel them. The books, the therapists, the family, the friends all help. But the secret I found was that, in the end, you have to make peace with the death of your loved one all by yourself. There is no one way to do it, all that matters is that you do it. You have to find your own way.

I always said that I was a law unto myself. I came to learn what that law within me was all about. The law within me was about love. I would have been nothing without the love I have had for Cece and my two sons. The one thought that guided my way during my grieving was that death happens to all of us, but love happens for the lucky ones, like me. If you have had love, it can never be taken away from you, not even by death. It endures in your memories and in your heart.

After two years had passed since Cece's death, I finally did what I knew she would have wanted me to do: I donated all of her clothes to Angel View Charities that takes care of crippled kids.

I knew Cece loved Palm Springs and how much she particularly loved our house. So after five years, I buried her urn in front of our house along with a statue of the Holy Angels. Cece didn't go to church, but she practiced in her heart her Catholicism. And I also placed with the urn and the statue a New York Yankees polo shirt, because Cece was a big New York Yankees fan.

I also put my marriage ring in there.

CHAPTER SEVENTEEN

Mailroom 2011

I was never really thinking about show business *per se*.

As a kid, I was never caught up in that. I started playing clarinet when I was eight years old and I loved playing it and being in the school orchestra. Things just evolved, and my proficiency on the clarinet got me into the High School of Performing Arts. Even then, my ambition was to be strictly a musician. Then I dipped my toe into booking bands, and I was hooked for life.

It has been a good life, essentially the life I saw for myself when I was that little kid growing up in the Bronx. I wanted excitement, fun, but I also wanted to accomplish something worthwhile. I wanted more than the world of my father.

When I was a kid, New York was thriving, energetic, glamorous. Everybody got dressed when they went out. Men wore suits, ties and hats. Ladies wore hats and gloves, sometimes hats with veils. Even if you were poor, you had one nice set of clothes.

Back when I was ten years old, I'd get a thrill on a Saturday night, taking the subway down to Times Square. I would just stand there, watching the crowds moving through the lights. That was New York. That was the good feeling everybody had. Guys had come back from the war. Guys were going to school. Guys were getting married, getting good-paying jobs. People got along. There was a job for everybody. Whether you were a machinist or accountant, there was a job for you somewhere. Everybody had a two week vacation. Things were just great.

It was still like this when I joined William Morris. Not only with William Morris, but with the agency business in general, there was a civility to it. Particularly at William Morris there was a family solidarity where everybody helped everybody else. If a guy got fired, you were in shock. If you were working there, you thought you were going to be there for life. There was no such thing as jumping ship for another agency because they were going to give you three dollars more. Nobody thought those things.

Even if you never met the guys working for WMA on the West Coast or in Chicago, you knew them because you communicated through memos. We communicated everyday with teletypes. There was a teletype operator who was a trainee. He had graduated from the mailroom. There was a big teletype room. You didn't send teletypes unless it was important. About two sheets of teletypes were sent to the West Coast every day. The West Coast also sent teletypes back to New York. Everybody had their own initials, just like e-mail today. The teletypes were the e-mail of the sixties.

An agent would put his memos in his "out box." There were inter-office memo envelopes with lines on them. The guy who got the envelope crossed out his name and put the next name of where the memo would go. The mailroom guys would not only deliver the mail, but pick up outgoing mail and put it into the boxes for Airborne to the West Coast. Airborne was the precursor of Fed Ex. Then Airborne would come by at night and pick up whatever bundle we'd put together of inter-office memos and take it to California. The next day, the West Coast office would get those inter-office memos. In the same way, the West Coast office would send inter-office memos to New York.

I went back to the William Morris agency about a year ago. One of the things I'm proud of: I trained a couple of guys who became very successful agents, one of whom was Rob Heller. He's still a hot agent on the West Coast for William Morris. There are a couple of others. So I went to visit these guys.

I was shocked at the lack of decorum and standards of dress there when I went into the offices at William Morris. We always had to wear a shirt, tie and jacket. We were allowed to at least wear a sport jacket and slacks, if necessary, but always a shirt and tie. Our competitor, MCA, was so strict with their dress code that their agents always had to wear a suit-- no such thing as a sports jacket-- and only a white or blue shirt. MCA even had a motto: "Dress British, but think Yiddish."

Now you go into the agencies, it looks like you're at a ballgame on a Saturday afternoon. Guys are working there with their sneakers, shirttails hanging out and jeans. It's not the same. The camaraderie isn't there. Each guy is out for himself. If they can get a better offer somewhere, they jump ship. It's very cut throat.

With us at William Morris in the sixties, if we didn't return a call in 48 hours, the bosses heard about it, and we got living hell from them. Today, it's commonplace for guys to *not* return calls unless they really want to return the call. If they don't know you, you won't hear back from them. Or if they don't think you're important enough, they won't return the call. It sort of feeds an ego with them. I don't understand whatever that is, but it's a commonplace thing today.

There was camaraderie with not only the other agents in the office, but with competing agents. There was a fun about it. Yes, we competed, but in a spirit of friendship. If I couldn't sell an act to a nightclub, I would call a competitor and say, "Hey Joe, so-and-so is looking for something. I don't have anything for him. Why don't you give him a call?"

Here's an example of the camaraderie we had:

One night I'm at the Copa, meeting with rough and gruff Julie Podell, the owner. Podell was drinking heavily and I may have said the wrong thing. He let me have it verbally with both barrels. He tore me apart, so much so that it was embarrassing.

Larry Gengo, who was with GAC, along with a couple of other agents from competing offices were waiting to take their turn to meet Podell. Gengo felt so sorry for me, standing there taking Podell's tongue-lashing, that he went into the men's bathroom of the Copa where he knew there was a public pay telephone, and he called the Copa's general number to page me, to get me away from Julie Podell. That's the kind of camaraderie and relationships you had with the guys you were competing with. But that's not today.

The price structures in show business today are completely out of whack compared to what they were years ago. Years ago if an agent was knocking out $40,000 to $60,000 a year plus profit sharing and bonus, he was doing well. Today agents are making a million, four million—- unbelievable! That's why nobody today cares about camaraderie or loyalty. They're just looking for that buck. The same thing with the pay scales of artists. It has all gone through the roof. Are the shows better today?

Well, I'm an optimist; show business will never die. It has changed from the days of Shakespeare to the opera to vaudeville to the motion pictures, radio and nightclubs to the Las Vegas casinos to the Indian Casinos to now—- if you're big enough-- to those enormous civic arenas. Who knows what tomorrow will bring with the Internet? Show business is big now, all right, and if it's going to be better, we've got to make it better.

If you've come this far with me in my story, I thank you. I think I had a story worth telling. I know it was a story worth living. Throughout my tale, I've mentioned my "Hands of Fate" stories. A lot of them have happened to me. I'd bet they've happened to you, too. Life takes a turn for all us at one time or another. I'd like to close my story with this true account of the Hands of Fate taking hold of my life:

I'm playing in the band at Grossinger's, in the Catskills. This was right after I graduated NYU and I wanted that last fling at being a musician before I would give up music altogether.

So we were allowed to eat the best food at the hotel because of the union. But after a while of eating hotel food every day, breakfast, lunch and dinner, you got tired of it. You wanted something different.

444

I said to the trombone player: "Come on. Want to go to Duke's?"

Duke's was a hot, Chinese restaurant in a neighboring town. We slept late, so this was after lunch and before dinner, three o'clock in the afternoon. We pull in to the parking lot, which was in the back of the restaurant. You parked your car and went in through the back entrance. The whole parking lot was empty. Nobody was there. So I pulled the car into a parking spot that was right next to the back entrance.

Don't ask me why, but I said, "You know, Joe? I don't think I like this parking spot. I don't know why."

I back the car up. I turn around, and I go to another spot some distance away, facing the other way.

Just as I pulled the car into the other spot, I looked up the hill, and said, "Jesus Christ! Take a look at that car coming down the hill! It's coming down awfully fast!"

This car was barreling down the hill in a

cloud of dust. It came rocketing into the parking lot and crashed right into the spot where we had just been parked.

If I hadn't moved the car, we would've been killed.

The woman driving the car said her brakes had suddenly failed.

What possibly could have induced me to decide to move my car?

I can only think: The Hands of Fate.

***

As an agent for William Morris, Larry Spellman discovered and signed such talents as Rodney Dangerfield, Anne Murray, Joan Rivers, Al Martino, Norm Crosby, Jack E. Leonard, David Frye, Billy Vera, The Kingsmen, and others, before establishing his own theatrical management firm and going on to film and theater production. Larry currently makes his home in Palm Springs, California.

Page 145 156, 160,

Made in the USA
Middletown, DE
10 September 2018